The Ultimate Digital Marketing Guide: SEO & Facebook

(2 Books in 1)

Matthew Bartnik

Book 1:

The Age of Digital Marketing:
Master the Power of Facebook Advertising for Insanely Effective Social Media Marketing

Matthew Bartnik

Introduction

There is a virtually endless pool of customers at your fingertips that you can tap into if you learn how to master Facebook Advertising and learn how to take advantage of all the resources and data that Facebook provides for businesses.

This book will teach you how to get started with Facebook Advertising.

You will learn:
- All of the different ways you can advertise on Facebook
- How to decide which form of advertising will work most effectively for your business and objectives
- B2C vs. B2B advertising on Facebook
- The pros and cons of using Facebook Ads Vs. Google Adwords and how you can use both for maximum reach
- How the platform works and how it automates your remarketing and targeting
- How to evaluate and learn from the facebook reports and data to optimize your marketing efforts and get the most bang for your buck.

You will become an expert in:
- Creating effective Facebook ads
- Exploiting the tools and tricks that most people aren't aware of on Facebook. This will give you a competitive edge

- Keeping your advertising campaigns lean by controlling the budget and spending only on the most effective strategies and campaigns
- Avoiding the 30 most common mistakes people make with Facebook Advertising.

This book is a comprehensive, step-by-step, beginners guide that will help you become an influencer on Facebook, a platform that is absolutely essential for marketers who want to be effective in the 21st Century.

Many people make the mistake of approaching Facebook Ads the same way they approach Google AdWords and other forms of paid advertisement. What they fail to realize is that people approach Facebook for completely different reasons than the reasons for which they approach google and other online platforms. When people are on Google and Amazon, for example, they're actively looking for information and are even actively looking to spend money on solutions to their problems. When people are on Facebook, they could be looking for information, but often they're looking for user-generated content, and entertainment. Thus, you need to completely re-orient the way you approach Facebook ads to efficiently reach the right customers in effective ways where they'll be receptive to your message. If you're just copying and pasting what you do for google ads, you're wasting your money. This is just one of the many ways people fail to adequately take advantage of and understand Facebook's robust advertising platform. This is one of the many issues that will be addressed later in this book.

We have all come in contact with Facebook Ads, whether we realize it or not. In this book, we will discuss the important facets of Facebook Advertising from what it is, whether it is important for your business, the how-to's, and many other great incentives that advertisers and marketers need to know.

It's 2018 and by now, you know that everywhere you look on the internet, you will be bombarded with ads. Facebook data is one of the most important ways 3rd parties collect information about consumers to effectively market to them. Facebook heavily influences people's online habits and Facebook ads, when used effectively, can be some of the most powerful tools to a digital marketer. So, what are they? We see them all the time, but do we know anything about them?

Here's a little info about Facebook Ads:

1. With Facebook ads, you are generally in control of your creative elements as you are the advertiser. This includes the title of the ad, the images used, the design, and the text.

2. Facebook ads use an auction type method wherein those who want to use Facebook ads are charged based on the clicks they receive, the impressions the ad gets, and the actions they results in. There are different formats of ads that Facebook offers which users can use.

3. You can craft and create all the different types of ads on your own or use Facebook's interface which enables you to self-service. If you need to work on your ads using a more wide-ranging tool, you can use certified API ad developers such as Qwaya.

4. Facebook ads can be categorized according to: i) Ads, and ii) Sponsored stories. Here are the different types of ads that you can create with Facebook ads. There are 10 kinds in total:

- Mobile App Ad

- Event Ad.

- Page post photo Ad

- Page Post Text Ad

- Domain Ad

- App Ad

- Page Like Ad

- Offer Ad

- Page Post Ads

- Page Post Link Ad

- Page Post video Ad

The places these ads will appear depends on the type you choose to use.

Facebook Usage Statistics

Believe it or not, not every business is on Facebook simply because they feel it is important to be interacting and engaging with their customers or target market on other social media channels like Twitter, Instagram, YouTube, and LinkedIn, and that may work fine for them. On the other hand, if you are planning to reach a wider audience, you might want to rethink and focus your marketing efforts to include Facebook as well. Here are some stats to enlighten you on the power of Facebook:

Usage Statistics

- Active users. On June 30, 2017, Facebook reached a total of 2.09 billion active, monthly users.

- There is an average of 79% of Americans use Facebook.

- There are 50 million businesses using Facebook Pages.

- A total of 22% of the world's population uses Facebook.

- Every minute, there are at least 400 new users signing up for a Facebook Account.

- There are at least 1.2 billion monthly active users engaging and communicating via Facebook Messenger.

- At least 83% of parents with children aged 13 to 17 years old are friends with their child on Facebook.

- Facebook is currently available in 101 languages.

Marketing Statistics

- 1 pm and 3 pm on Thursdays and Fridays are the most active times of usage for Facebook.

- Facebook Page content reach an average of 2.6 percent of organic reach.

- Pages that have smaller followings have a higher reach and higher engagement rates.

- Facebook is currently ranked as the most important platform for marketers.

- On average, brands post 8 times each day.

- 57% of consumers say that Facebook has influenced their shopping.

- User-generated content has more traction compared to brand-generated content, often creating a 6.9 times engagement rate.

- Finance and the Insurance industries have the highest cost-per-click on Facebook at $3.77.

- The apparel industry has the lowest cost per click at $0.45

- 93 percent of advertisers use Facebook ads.

- 4 to 15 words for a link description is the most effective length for ad titles on Facebook.

- Images make up to 75 percent to 90 percent performance for Facebook ads.

- $9.16 billion is Facebook's advertising revenue for 2017.

- 26% of Facebook users reported that they made a purchase after clicking on ads.

Facebook Marketing

Plenty of industry insiders who use Facebook understand its monetization models. However, not many understand how Facebook actually makes money.

Facebook has various revenue streams which include both past and future revenues.

The single most important revenue channel on Facebook is advertising. Facebook, at its core, has always been supported by ads since Facebook ad revenue regeneration is about half a billion each year. So, who pays for the advertising?

Self-Serve Facebook Advertising

Facebook's self-serve ad platform is where it gets its largest advertising revenue. You can literally start your own ad campaign on

Facebook by following its step-by-step guide. These ads are located at the sidebar on most pages on Facebook cover events, user profiles, groups, as well as third-party apps. Granular targeting is the primary advantage of this platform.

Over the past few years, Facebook has tried to make their advertising more targeted by offering things like limiting your ad to metropolitan areas, zeroing in on variable targets such as age, gender, workplace, school, relationship status, and specific keywords.

Facebook has also released its Facebook Ads API. This gives large buyers and managers the capacity to build comprehensively on top of their existing advertising platform.

This Facebook Ads API will mostly help advertisers who spend a large amount of money a day just for modifying existing ads and posting new ones. Currently, the largest purchaser of Facebook's self-serve ads is Zynga who is also the developer of the largest games on Facebook such as Cafe World and Farmville. Of course, there are other advertisers who contribute to Facebook's revenue such as restaurants, societies, pet shops, lawyers, and doctors.

Engagement Ads

A substantial percentage of income for Facebook is from Engagement Ads. These types of ads can be placed on the homepage of the website which is an ideal solution especially for big brand names.

Users who enter the website would be able to interact with these ads. These ads are commonly found in the brand's homepage on the right-hand side. Facebook is always striving to create more avenues to attract brand advertisers and marketers, and with the launch of Brand Lift, Facebook is definitely taking the ad game to a whole new level. With Brand Lift, advertisers can test huge campaigns and study and scale their effectiveness. Brand Lift is also designed to maximize the level of measurement. This will hopefully encourage the brand advertisers to shell out more money on Facebook Engagement Ads.

Virtual Goods and the Marketplace

Facebook also makes a large amount of revenue from its Market Place or even its Gift Shop feature. Through Gift Shop or Marketplace, users can buy and sell products to one another. Facebook Marketplace has generated almost $100 million in revenue which makes it a very lucrative business.

The Marketplace has become a place to even purchase gifts for victims of a tragedy. In 2108, Facebook can expect to generate about $180 million just from the Marketplace alone.

Facebook Credits

Facebook Credits Stream is another way where Facebook can generate revenue. This used to be the way Facebook users could purchase virtual goods through Facebooks Gift Shop, but since Facebook has opened up this option to third-party developers, Facebook credits cannot be directly added into applications such as Farmville.

Facebook is greatly expected to continue expanding its platform to offer marketers more and more ways to advertise. This expansion also means that brands can look toward growing revenue by leaps and bounds.

Section 1 Conclusion:

- Advertising still remains the revenue channel of Facebook despite it making revenues from other sources.
- Self-serve ads are still the number one choice of ads for any booming business. Facebook has been experiencing continued growth and is showing no signs of stopping any time soon. As long as advertising is bringing in the big bucks

for Facebook, it is unlikely that Facebook will start charging brands to open Facebook pages.

Chapter 1: Facebook Advertising versus Google AdWords

Many advertisers and marketers kept viewing Facebook Ads and Google AdWords in an adversarial way. It was thought that these two long-standing rivals were in direct competition with one another. Marketers were trying to see which one was best as if it was only necessary to choose one for their needs.

This is a false idea that until today is confusing and misleading in the online advertising avenue.

While you may think that these two big and brilliant brands are seen as competitors, the truth is, both of these brands co-exist. They serve different functions and many brands benefit from both Google AND Facebook Ads. What you should be doing when you want to achieve increased leads, maximum visibility, attract new customers, and acquire more sales is to leverage from the strengths of both Facebook Ads and Google.

For marketers and advertisers, you need to come up with different strategies that work on the strengths of each platform because this will bring in exceptional returns on your marketing expenditures. In this chapter, we will look into both of these types of advertising, the pros, and cons of each as well as which one you should consider using in your strategy on digital marketing.

Google Ad Words and Facebook Ads–The Difference

Before deciding anything, you need to familiarize yourself with the features of both these advertising platforms and also understand the fundamental differences between the two.

Google Ad Words: Paid Search

Currently, Google AdWords is the most popular of PPC (Pay-Per-Click) advertising. In the online advertising world, AdWords is what it is usually referred to as (and is so synonymous with) paid search. In paid search, the text-based advertisements as well as the specific keywords are used to describe a brand or a product.

Advertisers use AdWords to bid on keywords that are unique to their brand and that are commonly used by Facebook users to search brands, products, or services. By bidding on these keywords, marketers, and advertisers hope that their ads or business will come upon the user's search results.

The advertisers will get a certain amount of money when an ad is clicked by a user. This is what it means by "pay-per-click advertising."

Bid optimization and PPC bidding is a complex element in itself which you need to thoroughly learn in order to use. In its very essence, advertisers pay for the probability of finding new customers via keywords and phrases that they think users will potentially use when they look for things on Google.

Facebook Ads: Paid Social

Facebook ads can be categorized as "paid social" and they are one of the most prime examples relevant to today's online advertising world. Facebook has the distinction of having the highest quantity of MAUs or monthly active users and it is a profitable element of today's digital advertising repertoires.

While you can say that Facebook ads work similarly to the way Google Adwords works, the fundamentals are different and advertisers use both platforms to promote themselves on digital avenues. And this is where the similarity stops.

A business can use paid search to acquire fresh users utilizing the specific keywords. Users find businesses in paid social based on the things they are interested in or like.

The common difference between Facebook Ads and AdWords are:

Now that we have looked into the main composites of Facebook Ads and Google AdWords or in other words paid social and paid search, let's look into the strengths for each of these platforms and how these different tools can be used to your advantage.

The Benefits of Google AdWords

Google is the existing leader in online advertising, procuring the name of the most used and most popular search engine. Google amasses a total of 3.5 billion searches every single day. For marketers, Google is a gold mine that has an unequal and unprecedented pool of users who are always in search of goods and services to fulfill their needs and pain points.

They are divided into two main channels:

1. **The Search Network:** The search network is what Google is all about. Google is first and foremost a search engine and all its products are built around that fact. Advertisers can recommend several phrases and keywords to target potential clients and businesses.

2. **The Display Network.** This network is more visual with ads (especially banner ads) that are literally all over the internet. Visual banners are an excellent choice for advertisers whose main goal is not necessarily like those of PPC ads which are conversion-driven.

A Massive Audience

Google's advertising platform has an immense reach, and this is among the main advantages of Google. With each passing year, Google progresses on its technology and it gets more sophisticated as it goes. The search volume is likely to become more amazing, especially with Google's proprietary artificial intelligence such as RankBrain. When this happens, advertisers will also acquire potential users and clients. This potential will make Google a lucrative addition to an advertiser's marketing strategy. It is easy to see why AdWords is the most popular form of online advertising that is used on the PPC platform.

A Level Playing Field

A lot of people think that the advertiser with the largest advertising budget has the best advertising gains with Google ads. But that's not true. In fact, nothing can be further from the truth. The quality of the ads and their relevance is what AdWords focuses on and not so much on how much is spent by advertisers.

Users will continue utilizing Google to search for the things and events they like when they are familiar with the tool and the ads are relevant to the user. Because of this chain reaction, Google AdWords reacts to relevant and quality above monetary input. In this position, advertisers will work on ads that are optimized, relevant, and high quality, rather than the poorly made ads.

The amount advertisers need to bid will depend highly on the relevance and quality of the ads. Google has some metrics that are highly valued apart from click-through rates which are a well-thought-out and reliable assessment of ads' overall appeal and quality.

A Variety of Ad Formats to Choose

AdWords only had 350 advertisers when it was initially launched in 2000. These text-based ads were, at best, rudimentary alongside Google's search results, but the essential elements are still utilized in current ads. PPC and AdWords ads are largely text-based. With these types of ads, advertisers can have more exciting, compelling, and attractive ads to attract prospective users.

Site links, ad extensions, and social proofing such as location targeting, user reviews, and a slew of other amazing elements are available to advertisers and it offers advertisers unparalleled levels of control and customization.

The other feature Google has introduced is ad formats which cater to specific businesses like hotels, spas, restaurants, workshops, vehicle manufacturers, or computer stores. The advertising needs in some industries go beyond simple text-based ads. They also need ads with rich visual elements such as interactive map data or even high-resolution images.

There is a good chance there will be an ad feature no matter where you sell from or what you sell or to whom, that will make your products reach your desired target market. As Google continues to implement new ad formats and features, it will continue exporting marketers and advertisers to reach newer target audiences and drive their businesses to greater horizons.

The Advantages and Strengths of Facebook Ads

Facebook Ads, compared to Google AdWords, is a newcomer to the online advertising scene, but it has been refining and improving its solutions over the past years. Despite its newcomer status, Facebook Ads is now a pioneer in online advertising, especially in the area of paid social, and has become the norm in digital marketing strategies.

Unmatched Audience Granularity

At this point, Facebook can now proudly claim to have a vast international audience all over the world. There will be no rivals to Facebook in terms of the size of its audience since almost one-fifth of the earth's population is on Facebook.

Users share almost every detail of their lives on this platform, from marrying to meeting people, the food they eat, their children, and even career moves. From joys to accomplishments to milestones, Facebook users post about these things daily. They also search for and engage with content that aligns with their personal beliefs, interests, values, and ideologies, thus giving advertisers a unique opportunity to create advertising messages that best fit their target audiences in ways we never thought possible.

Among the most powerful features is the ability that allows advertisers to create "lookalike audiences." Customer information can be uploaded from the advertiser's databases to Facebook, and this information can then be filtered based on its own data and information, and delivered by third-party data brokers, to match users that the advertisers uploads.

This creates the "lookalike audience." Advertisers can sufficiently and effectively grow their possible reach of each ad by focusing on customers that show similar behaviors and interests shown by current users. The answer, by now should be clear. Yes, Facebook Advertising works extremely well and is beneficial. However, advertisers should not be viewing Facebook as a billboard but as a gateway to achieving a closer connection to their customers.

A Visual Platform

The other main difference between Facebook Ads and text-based Google AdWords is that Facebook thrives on beautiful images. In fact, it's not Facebook alone. Almost every social media today thrives on beautiful, visual content. The best ads on Facebook blend in beautifully with images and videos and other visual content. Powerful visuals enable advertisers to leverage strong and persuasive images and also make ads with the potential of going viral that are compelling, and high-quality which convey strong messages.

Facebook constantly experiments and evaluates the various ways they can offer better and more superior marketing needs to its advertiser, and a more rewarding and satisfying online experience for its users.

Incredible ROI

Marketers and advertisers using Facebook Ads are often in awe of the scale and level of detail of Facebook's targeting options, combined with the tools they have, for creating engaging and beautiful ads. Apart from that, the ROI (Return On Investment) on these ads is immense. Advertisers can definitely expand their ad budget to its maximum potential and get their money's worth on this platform. The ad campaigns on Facebook, however, are reliant on different factors such as messaging, scope, campaign objectives, and target audience. They are affordable and gives advertisers the kind of impact needed. The best part is the very specific and direct targeting it allows.

Facebook Ads' highly competitive pricing and amazing potential returns make it a very popular platform for small businesses and companies that have limited budgets. No doubt, Facebook Ads is the best online advertising solution for marketers and advertisers who value their investments.

Google Ad Words vs Facebook Ads: Where to Invest?

Google AdWords and Facebook Ads are powerful platforms for advertising, and suitable for almost every type of business in our 21st-century world. Both of these platforms should be seen as complementing each other in your advertising arsenal. This is important to take note of because many people approach digital marketing with an "either or" attitude when deciding between Facebook ads and Google Adwords. Both have a very important place in a digital marketer's tool belt.

Both the power of paid social and paid search should be utilized by advertisers in order to achieve more successful ads. An advertiser should have two advertising strategies in place that use the benefits of each platform. Marketing messages are best when kept consistent on Facebook Ads and Google AdWords. It is also important to understand how to tailor these messages, so you maximize the ROI and ensure business growth.

Facebook vs AdWords: What's Right for Your Business?

The good old days of PPC advertising were simple—you needed to get clicks on your ads to get money. For early adopters, AdWords was a game changer in online advertising—the traffic was good, the cost was even better. But over the past 10 years, the cost per click on AdWords has increased. In essence, AdWords can make you tons of money, but it can also make you lose loads of money.

As we know today, AdWords is not the only available and viable PPC solution. You have plenty of options where PPC advertising is concerned. So which one should you choose? Of the available options out there—Twitter, LinkedIn, Facebook, and AdWords, you should start with both AdWords and Facebook.

But which one is the right one for your business?

B2B Marketing

Let's begin with B2B (Business-2-Business) marketing. For B2B companies, AdWords works fantastically. B2B searches also incur high CPC (Cost-Per-Clicks), but the customer LTV (Lifetime Value) is also pretty high. You could pay $15-$25 for each click, but if the sale is

$10,000, then that is a CPC you can handle. Another beneficial acquisition channel is LinkedIn Ads but for now, the main brands we are looking at are Google and Facebook.

Facebook has also entered the B2B domain because it now also lets you create ads that can be refined to Job Title, Industry, Company Size, Job Role, Seniority, and Office Type. As an added benefit, you can also create lead ads which Facebook auto-populates with the user's contact information and allows you to add at least three additional fields to further identify the lead for your sales team.

For some companies though, these features also enable Facebook ads to become a better fit for their B2B efforts in advertising since these companies are mostly interested in generating top-of-funnel leads. In B2B advertising, the brunt of your budget will go to Adwords and LinkedIn but you should still portion off some of your budget for Facebook Advertising. The quality of B2B traffic and leads you get through Facebook, however, will be significantly lower than what you would receive from AdWords.

Retargeting

Despite how much advertising focus you place on Google or Facebook for your B2B, you must always remember to retarget on these platforms. You have already generated a significant amount of traffic to your site. You can continue this position of staying at the top of your user's mind during the sales process by simply retargeting. For both these platforms, it is always best to use different ads, so you do not end up with ad fatigue. With Facebook, in particular, it is also good to use a range of ad types such as video, single image, GIFs, and carousels, so that your ads are entertaining and fresh.

Facebook vs AdWords

The use of Facebook or AdWords for B2B is straightforward. You can start by investing 90% of your advertising budget on AdWords and the balance 10% on Facebook Ads. Allow the cost per lead and also ultimately cost per sale data decide on what that ratio would be.

B2C Marketing

When it comes to B2C (Business-to-Consumer), Facebook is the better option because of the cost-per-click. In B2B marketing, your LTV can easily absorb a substantially high CPC. However, with B2C advertising, it is much more cost-sensitive.

The cost-per-click for a B2C business on average would be $0.90. On the other hand, clients do pay around $8.00 for clicks on AdWords. Advertising on Facebook for B2C business is the same as going back to the days when Google clicks only cost pennies.

However, with Facebook traffic being higher-funnel-traffic compared to AdWords traffic, your Facebook conversion rate is also typically lower than your AdWords conversion rate. Despite that, your CPC is significantly lower on Facebook than with AdWords.

Where Facebook May Not Be the Best Option

In B2B, you'll find that Adwords campaigns usually perform better than Facebook campaigns, despite Facebook being a great option for B2C businesses. This also depends on the type of products and services you're marketing and the businesses you're marketing to. An exception might be small businesses and sole proprietorships. If you're marketing to small businesses and entrepreneurs, Facebook ads may perform better for you than Adwords.

Niche Products

It is a little difficult to make niche products excel on Facebook simply because Facebook marketing is as good as the data you provide. The target market for niche products is typically small regardless of which part of the funnel you're advertising in. Even when your ads get plenty of clicks on your niche product, you probably won't see the kind of sales conversions you want because Facebook's algorithm does not have that much data to work with.

Who sees your ads is dependent on Facebook's algorithm. So, the smaller your target audience is, the more difficult it will be for Facebook to drive the kind of traffic you desire and get the conversions you want through your Facebook ads. That said, Facebook is not a bad platform for niche products but between Facebook Ads and AdWords, the clear winner for higher ROI would be AdWords.

Expensive Products

Facebook clicks and conversions are thought to be impulsive decisions. People may see your ad but are not necessarily searching for your product. This is ideal if you are selling $30 earrings, but what if it's a new car?

While people will end up buying a new car, they are not necessarily looking for it on Facebook. People aren't typically on Facebook to shop. But if someone is searching for "new Toyota Hilux" on Google, chances are, they are ready to buy. The more expensive the product, the harder it is to get people to buy using Facebook Ads. They will likely click on your ad, but it does not necessarily turn into sales leads.

Allow Data to Decide

Weighing the pros and cons and reviewing the research for themselves, marketers should make the decision on which platform works best for them based on the data and the unique needs of their individual businesses. Your ROIs on your ads should be the deciding factor on how much to invest and how often to invest in Facebook Ads and AdWords.

Generally speaking, Google adwords will cost more and require a bigger budget, but they'll offer a better ROI. But if your customers are usually on Facebook, then that could be a more attractive option. Advertising on Facebook, despite the lower ROI, may get you into other essentials such as building brand awareness which then increases the additional search volume for ads through AdWords.

So, Which is Right for Your Business?

There are plenty of factors that lead to deciding which pay-per-click platform is the most suitable for your business and brand, but if you want to have some considerations, there are things that you can look into:

- B2B Businesses: Good to begin with AdWords and start to retarget on both Facebook and AdWords Display Network. Also, test Facebook for your business by investing at least 10-20% of your monthly ad budget.

- B2C Businesses: Good to begin with Facebook, unless your product is expensive, or it is a niche. In this case, start with AdWords and progress to Facebook. You also need to spend at least 10-20% of your ad budget to test on your non-primary market.

Chapter 2: Defining your Advertising Goals and Objectives

You need to look closely at the overall requirements of your business to create a successful online marketing strategy. In plenty of cases, an internet marketing strategy's effectiveness is undermined by a failure to measuring the elements that are required to understand the scale of success.

In this chapter, we will teach you to measure the efficacy of your current digital marketing strategy.

What Types of Campaigns are you Doing?

There are different outcomes for each type of internet marketing campaign. These outcomes will vary depending on different variables like the targeted customers, products, nature of the company, demographics, environment, and so on. You would have to ensure that marketing campaigns, newsletter campaigns, online advertising campaigns, and social media campaigns are all running concurrently.

You must know the types and number of campaigns that you will run. When you do these campaigns, you must concentrate on the budget for every campaign, its target audience, and so on.

How to measure the efficacy of your campaigns:

For every campaign that you run, it is crucial to measure its effectiveness. Almost all marketing campaigns need to be self-sustaining. This depends entirely on the approach used in digital marketing. You always need to remember that ineffective marketing campaigns can lead to financial loss, waste of resources and damage to your value proposition.

A marketer should measure the campaign's effectiveness against the company's achievements and fixed goals. For example, you can evaluate the growth rate of your business and measure how you compare against your competitors accordingly. Find your brand's value proposition, strategies for growth, goals, and marketing channels, as well as any under-utilized methods. See which of these best fits your requirement and profile.

What Tools do you use to Calculate the ROI of Your Campaigns?

ROI, or return on investment, is viewed as proof of the effectiveness of your marketing plan. Using a few simple tools can easily measure the ROIs. Also, using metrics usually can help measure ROI from:

- Customers: The most important entity for a successful business. Check and keep track of your customer conversion rates. The rate of returning visitors to a site is also essential to maintaining popularity and effectiveness of your campaigns.

- Conversion rates: This is the first element you need to look at. You need to define targets for online purchases, web visits, contact forms, newsletter subscriptions, and time spent on a page as well as user interaction on the site and user interaction on social media.

- Traffic: Measuring referral sources to check which strategies work efficiently through Google Analytics.

- Leads: Check your traffic from your blogs and websites and see which of these converts to leads. Focus on:

  o Bounce Rate.
  o Average page views per visit.
  o Average time spent on site.

- Audits: Social media audits also need to be conducted to measure reach as well as content effectiveness.

- Reach: Track to see how far and wide your posts and content are reaching, is the reach within your target audiences and is traffic resulting from this reach.

- Conversion Regularity: Keep track of the visit-to-lead conversions such as online traffic from leads.

- Costs: Costs to acquire customers or costs per lead is an important factor to measuring campaign effectiveness. Costs can be calculated by dividing the advert costs by the marketing costs with new and paying users that you have acquired during that period.

- A/B tests: Among the best processes to measure campaign effectiveness.

How do we Conduct A/B tests to Measure Effectiveness of Campaigns?

Decide what to test

Using A/B Testing allows you to test two pieces of content against each other. You can test something as minor as the color used for a CTA (Call-To-Action) to something as significant as a redesigned website page. When conducting A/B tests, you must only attribute the results to every piece of content that you are testing as a whole and not on individual or singular differences.

For example, if you are testing two versions of one landing page against each other, and you have made changes to the CTA copy, the form length, the images, and the heading on one of the landing pages, then you cannot attribute that landing page's success to the form itself. You have to attribute the success of it to all four elements that you have changed.

There are many items you can conduct A/B testing on. Let's take a look at what happens when running A/B Testing on what changing the colors of the CTA buttons can do.

Determine the Outcome of Your Test and Decide how you Want to Measure it.

To run an effective A/B test, you have to first identify the goal or result you want from the testing. When it comes to the colors of the buttons, let's assume your goal is measuring the effects of each CTA color on the response of the user who encounters the button. This is among the most straightforward tests that you can conduct. You can easily test this more than once with different colors. You can also test to see how changing the color would make it more visible on your website's real estate. In this example, we will look at the number of clicks on the CTA that send people to the landing page, as a success metric.

Set Your Control and Treatment

The control refers to Version A of your testing. This encompasses the usual elements that you use on a landing page, your CTA, your heading, and your email. Version B is the test subject. It includes the elements and changes that you want to test on. For example, the elements in Version A could be dark blue or light grey, which are standard colors used in most CTAs and blogs. However, in Version B, you want to change the color to bright green.

Create Your A/B test and Publish it live

Once you are done designing your experiment and deciding how it is going to work, it is now time to make it. Create the content for both Version A and Version B. In this example, Version A is the light grey button and Version B is the bright green button. The only difference in this example is the color. The images and copy used on both CTAs are the same. This way, we can only test the effects of the color and its correlation to the number of clicks.

Once this is done, you have to set up the test in your marketing software. Depending on the type of tool you use, the A/B testing can vary in its steps and it also differs according to the type of content to be tested. Here are some of the most common tools for A/B testing:

- Unbounce

- VWO
- Google Analytics Experiments
- Five Second Test
- Convert Experiment
- Maximiser
- Adobe Target
- AB Tasty

Promote Your Test to a Specific Audience

If you want your test to be statistically significant, you will need to promote your content extensively. Send your email and notifications out to a large list and promote your landing page across your social networks and blogs just to get enough people to see your tests.

Bear in mind that these tests are conducted to engage a specific audience, so you need to keep your promotions tailored to only that target market. For instance, you want to see if your Facebook followers will like something on a landing page, so only promote your content on your Facebook account but do not promote your A/B testing content anywhere else except on Facebook.

Gather data Until it's Significant

Once the testing is out, the waiting game begins. You need to consistently promote your test until it has reached a statistically large number. This is important because you can prove that your tests aren't determined by just chance alone. Once you have hit a significant number, you can see if Version B is more efficient than Version A.

But what happens if you never hit a statistical significance? You need to continue pushing promotions and wait it out for a few more days. Some A/B testing takes up to 30 days just to acquire enough traffic to obtain significant results. However, if after a month during which you've experienced significant traffic, you still have not seen any major results, then this testing hasn't made any huge impact on conversions. It is time to move on to a different type of testing.

Investigate Your Entire Marketing Funnel

If your experiment worked, great! But it isn't the end. It is time to look outside the test's original intention to see if it has any other effect on any other part of your marketing channels.

Some of the smallest details for a website or blog are some of the most effective in changing perceptions, increasing conversion rates, and so on. You may think that colors do not have any significant impact, but your tests show you that they do. You can also take your metrics one step further by looking at closed-loop analytics. With these, you can track to check if people who clicked on the CTA have turned into paying customers. Maybe the bright green call to action makes people become customers faster.

By looking at other factors beyond your massive campaigns, you can discover that an A/B test has other impacts and effects that you were not anticipating. If those impressions were good, then you can focus your attention even more on them. If they are not good, then you might want to change them.

Always remember that A/B testing can have larger implications than just the metrics alone.

Iterate on Your Findings

You have just finished your first A/B test, but do not stop there. There's so much more you can test. For example, in our CTA test, apart from changing the color, we can also change the location of the CTA on our website. Alternatively, modifying the copy of the CTA could also be done to see how users respond to it and click on it. You can also run your CTA of the same kind on a different timeline, date, during a holiday, and such so you can see the responses it brings. Testing your site can always help you tweak your campaigns and, in turn, bring in better conversion rates.

Simple Steps for Effective Online Marketing Strategies

1. Targets

In any marketing campaign, the first move is always to identify what your targets are. It is always good to focus on two primary goals and then two minor ones. All of these goals have to be ethical, have a timeline, easy to achieve, comply with the needs of the moment, and must be unique to the company.

2. Objectives

Setting specific marketing objectives keeps you focused on your goals. You can track your goals and accomplishments better by centralizing certain measurement metrics. For example, you will need a metric that determines the likes you receive on a successful target if increasing and influencing sales is one of your marketing objectives. Objectives can be categorized by measurability indexes, relevancy, and time.

3. Identification

Apart from defining your marketing aims and goals, it is also crucial to know your consumer's demographics and other essential profile information. For example, if you are conducting a community program, then it might be better to work on social network campaigns. If your target is the more mature groups, email marketing or even conventional marketing would do the trick and save you time and effort. Knowing your target market is very crucial for creating an online marketing strategy that has optimal results.

4. Market Identifiers

For any campaign, it is always good to stay ahead of your competition. If you know your competition is gearing up for a 50% discount sale for the holiday season, then don't be outsmarted by this. Tweak your campaign to offer promotions and discounts too.

5. Platforms

Pick and choose your social media. In any marketing campaign, overdoing your social media networks could mean death to your campaign. Before signing up and opening accounts for every network, understand your target group and choose your social media appropriately. Apart from that, choosing when to advertise on social media is also essential. For example, adults may engage more on social media during lunch hours or after work compared to teens who probably engage in social media longer.

6. Content Strategies

A good content strategy is valuable when combined with a proficient marketing strategy. Three vital components for content strategy are the number of posts per day/week, the time of day, and content type. There are periods of time that are suited for the types of social media posts. It is important to use this strategy and information when posting your products, service, or brand.

7. Marketing Techniques

As mentioned earlier in this chapter, tracking your marketing strategies has immense benefits. Tracking measures enable a marketer to identify what works and what falls short. Improvements can be made when we track our goals and objectives.

Chapter 3: Finding & Evaluating Your Niche & Your Audience

What is Niche Marketing?

Niche marketing is all about focus. It is a focus on selling and advertising your strategies towards a targeted portion of the market. You do not market to everyone who could benefit from your product or service. Your niche targets to specific people, focusing exclusively on a group of people or a demographic section of likely customers that would most definitely enjoy or benefit from your products.

Niche sectors stand out because of these reasons:

- Geographic area
- Lifestyle
- Occasion
- Profession
- Style
- Culture
- Activity or habits
- Behavior
- Demographic
- Need
- Feature reduction or addition

Niche marketing's biggest benefit would be that it allows brands to stand out from the pack and appear as unique. This ensures that your message resonates better with its already unique and distinct customer section. To build a lasting and strong relationship with your target audience and reach a higher growth potential, a brand should not blend in but instead be more valuable and stand out by employing niche marketing initiatives.

Finding Specific Niches Using Facebook

Advertising

Facebook has over 1.5 billion active monthly users. With this power, they can easily market to whomever they want. This is a huge opportunity for marketers and advertisers. But not everything is be perfect. Despite all that, some advertisers still find it hard to match their messages with the right audience.

While it is a good start to define your location, age, and gender for your ads, there is actually plenty more that you can do with Facebook Ads.

Here are other ways you can create a niche marketing using Facebook:

New Generations

In this era, you want to target the millennials and baby boomers. This group of audience is ideal for fashion, gadgets, clothing, and gaming.

People with an Upcoming Anniversary

Have something new to sell? You can reach to a target audience that is celebrating a special day such as an anniversary of any kind—work, birthday, or wedding. These groups are great for selling greeting services, flower deliveries, event planners, recreational activities, holidays, and restaurants.

People who have High Technology Adoption

If you are selling something that is either too high-tech or the opposite, target your audience following their technology exposure.

Niches by Household Members

You can also target your ads to hit people who live with a family member or have separate households. These groups are perfect for selling kitchen accessories, furniture, home appliances, and cleaning services.

Friends of People with Anniversary

We targeted people who are celebrating an upcoming anniversary but what about their friends and family? A reminder that a loved one's anniversary is coming up is the perfect time to sell online gift stores, eCards, eGreetings, party suppliers, and greeting services. These people are usually friends and family of the people who have upcoming birthdays and anniversary celebrations.

Small Business Owners

Small business owners are among the biggest groups or pages in Facebook. You can reach a wide demographic of customers if you are in the insurance sector, banking, or just selling your products and services on a small scale such as web hosting, web designing, and even small-time catering.

Target People who have a New Job

Target those who have landed a job! You can target them if you are selling clothing (they need office wear!), fashion, online learning platforms, management software, and eBooks.

People in new Relationships

You can create a niche for your advertising by narrowing it down to target people that have recently become engaged or just got married! You can sell greeting services, bouquet deliveries, flowers, eCards, event management, and restaurants.

People that create Events on Facebook

You can target people that have recently created an event on Facebook because this can be a great business for event management companies and party planners. This is also great for caterers, party supply companies, decorators, music and entertainment providers, and booking and registration services.

People who have Traveled Recently

People who have just returned from traveling can bring in big business especially for post-holiday services such as photo albums, photo editing software, GoPro video editing software, and graphic icons. You can also advertise medical services for those who have returned back from holidays as well.

Soon-to-be Parents

Couples who are about to be new parents will have loads of things to buy from baby strollers, baby toys, books, and also looking into preschool admissions and insurance. This is a major target audience that you can target for your niche marketing.

Reach People Using Facebook Payments Platform

This niche is a must-have for a business that is selling on Facebook or has linked third-party paid apps to Facebook. This feature enables marketers to reach all the audiences that have recently made a payment or are high spenders or people that have used the payment feature at least once. This is great for app developers, e-commerce sites, online retailers, as well as Facebook pages that sell stuff.

People Based on Their Technology Interest

Targeting people based on their interest in technology is the ideal way to ensure that these groups get the messages you want them to know. If you are selling computer devices, or you are launching a new app, or having a discount sale on consumer electronics, these are the kinds of things people, who like and use tech tools and gadgets, will want to know. Advertisers from the cell phone industry, computer hardware or software as well as e-commerce stores can fine-tune their marketing strategy to hit these customers.

People Based on their Political Interests

Facebook Ads can definitely help you segment out and reach audiences based on their political alignment. This is great for marketers who want to send out political party events, meetings, town hall discussions, and media houses.

Users Based on the Browsers they use

Browsers are one of the main ways Facebook knows what you are searching for. You can target your ads based on what browser your audience usually uses, whether it is a safari extension or a chrome extension. This is extreme laser targeting and would be useful for developer tools, browser extension developers, and productivity apps.

Users who have Responded to Your Event

People who are interested and answered to your event definitely means they like something about your event and may be interested in similar events. If you are an event creator, trade show organizer, or webinar organizer, you can create your niche with this audience type.

Users Based on Their Email Domain

You can also use Facebook Ads to target people using specific email domains such as Gmail or Yahoo or AOL. This is perfect for advertisers who sell auto-responders, email apps, or email marketing apps.

Target People Living Away from Home

There's always that group of people you can target that are away from home and homesick. There are many services that can benefit people who are living away from home such as money transfer businesses, fashion, travel, airline ticketing agencies, and e-greetings. Even immigration consultants can benefit from niche marketing like this.

Mobile Devices by Brand

Mobile device targeting is a must for any marketer as it enables you to target audience based on the type of mobile device they are using. This is ideal for mobile accessories stores, mobile app developers, as well as cell phone companies.

Friends of Users That Like Your Page

Birds of a feather flock together, no? The likelihood of a person engaging with your ad if their friend has also engaged with it is high. Utilize Facebook Connections Targeting to focus on this niche of targeting people who are friends of the people who like your page. Page owners of any kind of business will benefit from this kind of niche targeting.

Evaluating the Profitability of Your Audience

Tip #1 – Brainstorming:

Brainstorming is always effective for practically anything you need to work on—ideas, solutions, methods, and finding the right niche. To begin brainstorming ideas for your niches, meet up with your business partner or like-minded friends, who will be able to help you or someone you trust. Friends and family, who know you and your business partner are ideal. Next, you want to block off time to focus on your brainstorming; set a meeting, time, and date for this.

When you meet, one of the things to think about is the items that you or your business partner or friends have bought online or recently purchased. Write these things down, even if it perplexes you. There will be tons of niches that are profitable but that does not mean you should rush into the business of dropshipping.

When you have your niches, write them down and filter them according to:

- Competition: Look out for other competitor stores and look into the kinds of products that are oversaturated.
- Loyalty: Look at how users interact with brands they are loyal with. Scan comment sections because there are bound to be users who comment how long they have been using a product or service.

Tip #2 - Research, compare, and evaluate trends

eBay is one of the places to check whether items sell online. Once you get onto eBay, one of the things you want to research is identifying products in the different niches in higher-priced bracket, the ones that are expensive, so it can be anything like $50 or $200 or $500 depending on the product. When you get your search results, allow it to show "completed listings." Completed lists shows items in red or green, red being the item did not sell and green is sold. Look at the items only for the ads you are considering to niche in. It is okay to go over this list a few times until you identify about 20 products within your niche that sell out almost always, at least 10 units a day.

Tip #3 - Utilize Amazon

Being the world's largest retailer, Amazon sells everything imaginable. Because of this, Amazon is one of the best tools on the Internet for evaluating your ad and other amazing possibilities that you never thought of. Amazon is also a great place to help you in a specific niche as well by identifying the ad that sells the best. You can also choose "best sellers" from the navigation bar located at the top of the page right under the search bar. You can see all the ads that are shown or the products that are currently selling the best.

Tip #4 - Put on your Marketer Cap

You want to make a profit for any kind of venture or business you are in. So, you will most likely look into ads that create a successful profit line. To help discover what your target audience is talking about, here are some questions you can ask:

- What kind of blogs and websites do they interact with and visit the most?
- What kind of pages or accounts do they follow on social media?
- Which online stores do they usually purchase from?
- What do you think are their biggest obsessions?
- What kind of products do they usually collect or buy most frequently?

Tip #5 - Google Trends

Yes, Google Trends is another tool you can use to evaluate if your niche is profitable. What you want to look out for are niches that have stable growth, no matter how slight. Here is a list you can check out on Google Trends.

Tip #6 - FB Search

Facebook search can help determine the amount of engagement your posts actually get. You can also use this as a competitor analysis tool, so you can see what kind of posts both your competitors as well as customers make. You can also look up at the brands that are within your niche. Search using specific keywords.

Your search will turn up information based on people, pages, photos, videos, links, and marketplace. When you look at these pages, you can see the number of followers. It will also help you understand the kind of frequency your Facebook posts need to be following, which is somewhere between 1-2 posts per day to have a competitive advantage and scale quickly. Browsing the pages that come up in your search also gives you an idea of the direction of your marketing strategy. Looking through photos helps you understand the kind of material you need to create and the markets you can target.

Continue Your Research

You want to make sure you have an audience for your niche even before you were spending hours marketing and buying ads online. Here's a quick list of what to look for:

- What kind of social platforms do people market your niche on?
- Are there dedicated Facebook groups for your niche?
- Are there targeting options you can use on Facebook for this niche?
- What kind of forums exist for people to discuss the niche?
- Do people host events for this niche?
- Do influencers post about this niche?
- Are there fans for your niche?

Pinterest, YouTube, Instagram, and of course, Facebook, are all popular places to look if your niches are talked about on these platforms. It is always better to put your content where it is seen, heard, and speaks because this is where your audience spends time.

Another thing is, all these platforms have one element in common. They are all heavy on visuals which means, stunning images and video reach out to your audience faster.

Tools to Use to Evaluate the Profitability of Your Niches

A. Checking on Amazon for Profitable Niches

With Amazon, you can see the number of reviews a product gets which is a huge sign that it is profitable. All you need to do is enter your own niche and ideas and see what the results give you. If there are tons of products with plenty of reviews, that is a good sign your product and your ad will be seen. It is said that for every 1 review seen on Amazon, that translates to 10 to 1000 people having purchased the product because not everyone is going to write a review.

Take note of the average number of reviews the customer has on a product on the first page itself. This is for reference later, so you can craft an ad that speaks to your customers. Ideal markets are the ones that do not have one single product to sell but have plenty of options you can give your customers over and over again. Look for related products that you may be able to sell again too. Put in the ideas and take note of what product type sells best based on the reviews they get. This will help you in promoting your own products later.

B. Checking ClickBank for Profitability

If your niche is includes digital products, you can also use Clickbank.com to check your profitability. As the largest retailer of digital products on the internet, ClickBank can show you how many products out there match your digital niche. When you search for a product, write down the number of searches you get for reference purposes. Look also for the type of digital products people are purchasing such as info-products, eBooks, software, and even memberships. If you see 3 to 4 products in your searches, it is enough to know that there is a demand.

You can also look for "Gravity" on ClickBank. The Gravity number is a unique ClickBank algorithm that calculates the number of unique affiliates that have sold at least one item of the product in the past 7 days. The higher the number of gravity, the more affiliates there are promoting and making sales.

This tells you that the product is profitable and also popular. When you see loads of products in the niche you are in which also has high gravity score, this shows you that affiliates, like yourself, are making money off this product.

C. Finding Profitable Affiliate Programs on ShareASale

ShareASale is an affiliate network that enables independent companies to run affiliate programs. This allows consumers to also promote their products. You would need to sign up and verify your account before you can start using their site to browse affiliate programs. Once you are in ShareASale, you can find over 1,000 affiliate programs from independent merchants that include big names such as ModCloth, Reebok, NFL, OptinMonster, and many more. Click on Merchants, then Search for Merchants, and you can enter your niche idea in your search box. Click on products before clicking the blue button. You can then see the number of products and the merchants related to your niche. If you see plenty of merchants and tons of products, then you've found a profitable niche.

D. Using Commission Junction to Check for Profitable Niches

Also known as CJ.com, this is quite similar to ShareASale. This site also allows businesses to host their affiliate program. Here, you can see big brands such as VistaPrint, TripAdvisor, Verizon, and Zappos. This website also requires you to verify your business and sign up.

Click on "Advertisers" and then key in your niche idea in the "keyword" box. Just like the ShareASale site, if you see thousands of retailers and numerous products related to your searched keywords, then you have a goldmine staring back at you. This shows there's a customer demand.

E. How to Use Google to Find Other Signs of Profitability

Of course, Google is also a great place to find products that are profitable. You can also find products on sale which may not turn up in your research using the affiliate networks. You can search for something like "niche + affiliate program," niche being the product of your choice, and see what the results bring you.

F. How to Use OfferVault to Validate Your Niche Ideas

One way to validate your niche ideas is to use www.offervault.com where you can also search for affiliate programs that are within your niche and see the CPA (cost per acquisition) offers. CPA offers mean you are being paid for sending a lead, or in other words getting customer's information rather than making a sale. This is a different thing altogether, but for now you can use this to search your niche and see the results that come out. Not every niche is a good product for CPA offers, so there may be a chance you will not see your product here. But do not be discouraged. Some networks show the same products while some show different things depending on the algorithm of the site.

G. Are Products on Sale?

When you see certain products on sale and you see them on many different networks, these are signs that these products are selling well. This also means you have a profitable niche, and you can definitely make money from it. This also means that investing in ads on Facebook will enable Facebook to pull out as much data as possible to reach your target audience.

Conclusion

Now you need to go through all data from whatever you have been researching and all the positive signs you have gathered. When you look at these factors, the numbers will give you a very conclusive idea of whether the market you are in is profitable. Profitable niches usually have these common traits:

- High levels of people searching for your niche.
- Plenty of products that sell well.
- Plenty of people paying to advertise said niche.
- Loads of activity online from forums, blogs, Facebook groups, and other social media chatter.

There is money to be made if you see these positive results.

Chapter 4: Paid Ads vs. Creating Free Content on Facebook

Facebook Ads vs. Boosted Posts: Which Should You Choose?

This question is very common among the admins of Facebook pages. Even if you are new to a page, you are bound to see Facebook's prompt to "boost a post." This usually comes in when Facebook detects high activity on a certain post or if its algorithms have found other pages with similar content boosting a certain type of content that matches yours. The ability to boost your post is a very simplified addition to Facebook Ads' system. This system is designed to be simple and easy to use even for a non-marketer or advertiser.

However, simple doesn't always mean better. Boosted posts come at the cost of significant customization the complete ad system provides. In this chapter, let's look at the difference between boosted posts of Facebook campaign ads so you can decide which is best for your business and when to use paid ads.

Why Have Boosted Posts on Facebook?

With boosted posts, advertisers have the choice to use a post that has already been posted any time and promote it. When boosting a post, page admins can choose their target audience, decide on a budget, and how long the boosted post should run. This can be done on any post on your Page's timeline.

Facebook Ads vs Boosted Posts

A post that is boosted focuses on increased visibility for that particular post and more engagement. Boosted posts are great for brand awareness., and an increase in engagement can add value to social proof. An increase in engagement can also mean a lower CPA or CPA. You could also end up with more results with the same value of the investment.

With Facebook's recent update, you not only can increase engagement for that particular post, you can also choose the outcome of it, whether you want people to visit your profile more or visit your site. If this is your option, compared to increasing engagement on the post in terms of likes or comments, your ad should be visible to people who will most likely end up clicking. This option is available only if your boosted post has a link in it.

Changing the Objective of the Ad

Boosting posts right now is much simpler, and Facebook admins do not have or need to make many choices. For smaller businesses, who make up a big percentage of Facebook pages, this is preferable. With a few simple clicks, you already have a boosted post.

Boost Posts Interface

Boosted posts are much more limited than the full Facebook Ads system. There are some other things that you need to do on Facebook Ads compared to boosted posts. This includes:

- Having plenty of objective options.

It is important to define what your ad objective is at the start as this will help you determine what your campaign should be about. Posts that are boosted will allow you to focus on whether you want to increase engagement or increase website clicks. On the other hand, full systems will allow you to determine a specific objective whether it is conversions, store visits, or lead generation. Boosted posts do not allow for these types of campaign objectives.

- Campaign types.

Identifying your campaign types is imperative because Facebook will use this info to focus your ads on users who have the higher likelihood of taking the kind of action you are optimizing your ad for. This is determined based on the user's history of activity.

- Choosing detailed placement options.

When you decide on boosted posts, you can uncheck or check an Instagram placement whether on desktop or mobile. This includes Facebook's side ads and news feeds, Instagram stories and feeds, articles, messenger ads, as well as audience network ads. You can decide if you want your campaign to be shown for desktop users or mobile users only.

- Allowing for more targeting customization.

When it comes to boosted posts, you cannot use multiple audience types. For example, you cannot custom your audience and also add interest targeting. You can do this and so much more using Facebook ads. With Facebook Ads, you can customize by doing the following:

1. **Enabling manual bidding:** You can conduct manual bidding through Facebook Ads. You can choose either a maximum-per-bid rate or a maximum average bid. You can also choose what you want to pay for, whether clicks or impressions. Since you are able to choose these methods to scale your Facebook Ads, this is a significant but small feature to know if you ever choose to use it.

2. **Bid settings:** You can create carousel ads, ad descriptions, ad headlines, and choose the call to action button that would work best for your ads. These are the different creative and formatting options that you can do through Facebook ads but not through boost posts.

3. **Gaining additional creative control:** You can also add in your own headlines and targeted descriptions and choose a CTA that will work efficiently with your ads. These formatting options are not available when it comes to boosted posts.

When to use the full Facebook Ads vs Boosted Posts?

Facebook Ads, about 99% of the time, are the most obvious choice for most marketers as it offers much more flexibility in crafting the right ad to hit the right audience. You can even customize the exact objective you want your ad to achieve, and it can be optimized to give you the results you want.

You can also create video awareness campaigns via Facebook Ads. You can also do retargeting towards the 75% of people who have watched the video and target them with a lead ad that is automatically filled out with their information. Once they become conversions, you can then focus on retargeting users who have visited your site and show them similar items to what they are interested in buying with a carousel ad that has high-conversions.

When should I use boosted posts?

Boosted posts work amazingly in very specific conditions. Here are the circumstances that boosted posts work well:
- When you want to maximize visibility on a specific post.
- When you want to build social proof.
- When you want to create brand awareness.
- When you want to create profile awareness.

Examples on when boosted posts work amazingly well:
- When announcing a specific event and you want to increase attendance for that event as well as do social proofing at the same time.
- When you have a major announcement such as a launch, a release of a product or service, or even a grand opening, and you want more engagement and visibility.

- When you have shared user-generated content and you want to win over customer's trust and gain new followers.

When you need a quick engagement boost to help with your social proofing or if there is a specific message you want users to see, your best bet is boosted posts.

However, if you want a full-fledged ad campaign that gives you better customization to reach a specific and wider group of users and match with your campaign goals, then Facebook Ads is the way to go. There is no right or wrong with using either boosted content or Facebook ads. The only consideration is what your goals and objectives are and matching the right method with the objective you want to achieve.

Pros and Cons of Creating Paid Ads vs. Creating Free Content to Encourage More Organic Growth and Traffic

Let's be honest. It is difficult to get people to your business, whether you are doing this virtually or physically. If only it was that easy to just push a button and the right customers just show up. But alas, life is not that way. It takes effort, intelligence, and pairing the right tools to attract your customers.

Whether it is driving traffic to your site with Google Ads or Facebook Ads, or reaping traffic through social media, blogging, or email marketing, you are paying for your traffic either with money or time, or both.

The question here is not necessary if you want to pay for Organic traffic versus Paid Traffic since you will be paying either way. The ultimate question here is which will be more worth the effort, time, and money.

1 - Pay-Per-Click vs. Organic Traffic

Organic Traffic really just means traffic coming in via organic search. Organic search is only from search engine results. This literally means a user goes on a browser of their choice, looks for whatever product and service they want, and when the search results come in, they then click on whatever links they want, which will direct them to a specific site.

While this is organic, advertisers and marketers can still influence this decision. But most often than not, organic traffic already knows what they want and have made a decision the split second they click on search. It is only a matter of deciding which link to click on.

Pay-Per-Click Traffic, also known as PPC, this traffic is a result of users clicking on an ad that you paid to be placed at a specific location on the internet. Almost every platform or search engine allows you to set up advertising campaigns that you only pay based on the number of times people have clicked on your ad. You decide how much you want to pay and the ad service you use will charge you until the funds you have stipulated run out. You can also set up an ad runtime which charges you based on the clicks that happen during a time period.

The location of the ads or placement is entirely dependent on several factors such as the ad relevance, the bidding process, and the desired audience response. The position your ad takes on a page is directly dependent on the performance of the ad or the bids. Where PPC is concerned, you are simply utilizing a middle person, and in this case, the ad platform to link your website with to the other people who wouldn't access your site.

2 - Organic Traffic Benefits Vs. PPC Traffic Benefits

Most of the time when people use a search engine to look for certain products and services, they do not intend to click on ads. 70% of link searches are usually organic and that is consistent with organic traffic.

Organic Traffic Pros:

Positive Bias: The biggest benefit of organic traffic is that they will click on links that they already trust to find what they need. If you rank high on a search engine result, that means the user already has a positive perception on your site and trust that you are an expert in the industry.

However, you really need to be at the top for this perception to be present. This is where organizations and businesses use SEO to ensure that they are at the top 10 of a search engine result, specifically Google. Google is the gold standard simply because they have a large share of the search engine market. Google creates the SEO rules; other search engines follow suit.

What Google does is weed out spam and give users who use their engine the best content there is. When doing this, Google has consistently improved and changed their filtering system in order to provide the best quality content on the World Wide Web.

The SEO game is built on the quality of a site, its relationships with other websites, as well as the traffic flow to that site. Of course, it is much more than that when it comes to Google algorithms such as quality images and a responsive site. The main focus here is the quality of the content.

Encouraging Improvement: Before you begin an organic traffic campaign, you must already have built a site with great content. When there is no content, there will be no traffic and no search engine result ranking. Your ultimate goal is quality which will keep bringing people to your site, especially if your marketing objective is to be ranked higher in search engine results. SEO enables you to stay high on the ranking list and with better content, you can always be at the top. Great content needs to be on all pages of your site. This will not only optimize your site for search engines but also improve your customer's user experience, satisfaction, and increase brand awareness and favorability.

Organic Traffic Cons:

Time: The cost of organic traffic is, of course, time. You would need to spend a decent amount of time to wait for organic traffic to pick up. People need to know that you exist in order to want to find you. Depending on your strategy for search engine optimization, this can take a few months or even years if you want to be on the first page of search results. You may not have that kind of time to boost your website traffic.

Resources: Organic traffic also requires an immense amount of resources, but the good thing is there are also plenty of free tools on the internet to help you optimize your site to attract organic traffic. Knowing what kind of tools there are and how to use them is essential in your marketing arsenal

PPC Traffic Pros:

PPC traffic is an excellent source of traffic and if you create outstanding paid ads, you will see the kind of traffic build up. It appears that selected top positions will get an average click-through rate of 7%. Those looking for brand specific or product specific searches will also see your ad, which will increase the click-through rate compared to organic traffic.

You can definitely pay an agency to search engine optimize your site. There are plenty of services that do this, but it does take time to see results. However, PPC traffic is faster than unpaid organic traffic. Once you have paid and secured your spot at the topmost ranking, that spot is yours until some other site comes up and has a powerful SEO that pushes you down. Whatever it is, the likelihood of you being at the top 3 or even at the top 10 will still be there unless you stop optimizing your site or doing any other marketing or advertising initiatives.

Tailored fit: The ads that you pay for will also be tailored to meet your objectives and hit the specific audiences. Through PPC ads, you can target your customers as well as potential customers in ways that organic traffic cannot do.

If you do not measure the intent of the user when you pick your keywords for SEO, you probably will not get the kind of customers you want. PPC advertising does reach out to segments that you may not have covered through your organic SEO methods. With PPC, you can target audiences by age, marital status, income even, education level, and even hobbies.

PPC Traffic Cons:

Money: The problem with many things in this world is the lack of money. Without enough budget, your best option to increase traffic is by sticking to organic traffic. If you want to generate tons of leads in a short amount of time, then PPC is the way to go and you need to put in a serious amount of cash for this to happen effectively. However, the great thing with paid ads is that you can turn them off whenever you have what you need.

Both paid and organic are essential to your site. There really isn't the perfect way. Both methods bring in traffic in different ways, and usually a good ad campaign takes advantage of both organic as well as paid traffic to create brand awareness and visibility as well as drive traffic to your site.

Chapter 5: Building a Company Facebook Page

Facebook is one of the most popular free social networking sites that allows users to create profiles, upload content from photos and videos, send messages, poke friends, and keep in touch with other people.

To open an account, all you need to do is go to **www.facebook.com** and click on sign up. Next, put in your first name, surname, an email address, and a password. You are also required to fill in your birthday and identify your gender. Once you're done, Facebook will send a verification email to the email address you provided, you verify your account, and just like that, you are a registered Facebook user!

When we talk about Social Media marketing, Facebook has a special account catered to businesses, and this is called Pages. To open a Facebook page, you must first have a private Facebook account, and in this case, it's the account you opened up earlier. This is your own personal Facebook account—your Pages account is exclusively for your business.

How to open a Facebook Page?

Below is a series of simple steps to follow to open a Facebook page.

Step 1: Choose a Page Type

Head over to **https://www.facebook.com/pages/create.php**. You need to click on what selection best fits your business needs. These types are:

- Local Business or Place.

- Company, Organization, or Institution.

- Brand or Product.

- Artist, Band, or Public Figure.

- Entertainment.

- Cause or Community.

If you are a business that serves your community, then number 1 is your best category, but if your business serves a whole county or the entire world, then number 2 is your category. Since we are talking about Social Media Marketing, for this tutorial, let us focus on option number 2, Company, Organization, or Institution.

When you click on Company, Organization, or Institution, Facebook will require you to specify the type of your company by choosing a category. This can be anything from a political organization, food & beverage, community organization, Preschool, School, Small Business, or Travel and Leisure.

You are also required to provide a company name. We recommend that you follow exactly the business name that you have registered it under. Facebook allows you to only change your business name and URL once, so make sure you make the right choice.

Step 2: Fill in the Basic Information

By completing the first step, Facebook will then automatically walk you through four primary sections of information, which will provide the foundation of your Page. You need to give a short description of your company within two to three sentences. This will be the main introduction to your site. Make sure this information is the same as what is shown on your website or your objectives. The great thing is, the content on the About page can be revised.

Personalize your URL so that it's easier to promote your

Facebook page on other material and sites as well as on your website. A confusingly long URL isn't going to make it. The URL should mirror your Page's name or Business name. For example, if your business is Delia's Homemade Cakes, then your URL can be **www.facebook.com.deliascakes**

A profile picture is a must. Being a business page, uploading a logo for your business is the right step. Your profile picture will serve as the first visual icon for your page, so make it identifiable and the same with all your other online presence because you want to increase brand recognition. Anything you publish on your page or comment to other sites will have your profile picture. A square image works best, in the size of 180 x 180 pixels.

Fill in your contact details and include a cover photo as well. Once you are done, Facebook will also prompt you to advertise your new page. However, do not do this immediately—regardless of whether a paid advertisement is part of your strategy or not. There is no point having paid advertisement when you do not have compelling content on your page. So, before you click to subscribe, work on getting relevant material on your page first.

Step 3: Getting Acquainted with the Admin Panel

The good thing about Facebook is that it is extremely user-friendly. Once you are done providing all the relevant information, you are one step further in providing a solid foundation for your Page. Your Business Page is now LIVE! But don't share it to your personal feed or suggest it to your friend's list just yet. You do not want to do this until you get good content up.

On your page, look for "Settings." Click it, and you will see two panels. On the left are the various setting categories and on the right are the different items you can edit or change. In here, the most important things you need to change/edit or add are the Page Info, which basically tells people about your business. You can also change the Notifications to determine how you'd like to receive Page alerts.

The most important feature is the Page Roles. This function allows you to decide who the primary manager of the Page should be, and who can be editors or contributors.

Step 4: Adding Strategic Content

When it comes to content, Facebook allows six different types of content uploads which are:

- Plain text status.

- Photo with caption.

- Link with caption.

- Video with caption.

- Event page.

- Location check-in.

For the first post, go with a status update to say hello and perhaps an update on the latest project you are working on. Down the road of your social media marketing campaign, be sure to use a variety of content to engage, educate, and connect with your audience. Once you are done with uploading your profile photo, make sure to update your cover photo too. The cover photo helps attract people to your Page.

Now that you have content on your page, you can invite friends first, and then your colleagues and your acquaintances that you know can create some initial activity. You can also encourage your customers now that you have some form of activity on your page.

Step 5: Measure your Progress

Insights by Facebook are a great tool for Facebook Pages. This feature allows you to monitor the activity of your visitors based on the content you have uploaded. You get to see the page views, page likes, reach, and engagement over a certain period of time. You can also see what type of activity it is:

- Organic: the number of people who visited/clicked/liked/shared/viewed your post without unpaid distribution.

- Paid: the number of people who visited/liked/clicked/shared/viewed your post as a result of viewing your ads.

Insights will also tell you which posts have a higher engagement, reach, and the time with the highest activity. All this valuable data will enable you to craft future messages to target an even greater correspondence. It will also tell you which items work, and which don't. With Insights you can view:

- Overview: This tab shows you the overall activity within a 7-day timeline, such as page likes, post reach, and overall visitor engagement.
- Likes: This tab will show you the growth and losses of your fan base. You will also see the performance of paid posts and organic posts.
- Reach: This tab shows you the organic number of people your posts or page reaches every day. Once a week, check this statistic to see if there are spikes in your data and cross-check it to see what you posted that day.
- Views: This tab tells you where your visitors are coming from, like from another website, an article mentioning your business, another Facebook account, and so on.

And with that, you now have a Facebook Page!

Chapter 6: Biggest Mistakes People Make with Facebook Ads

Facebook advertising campaigns can feel like a Minesweeper Game—sometimes you hit your target and get the gains you want, and sometimes you hit a snag and things don't work out the way you hoped. Sure, it takes trial and error with ads to see which ones work and which don't, but mistakes come at the expense of time and money. So, in this chapter, we will look at rookie mistakes to avoid when it comes to Facebook Ads.

1. Targeting Mistakes

You may have stellar ad copy, a beautifully designed ad, and exceptional ad placement, but if it is seen by an audience that does not want what you have to offer, there will all be for naught. A research conducted by AdEspresso in 2016 found that there is a possibility of over a 1000% difference in the ads' cost-per-click depending on the audience you're targeting. For instance, the cost-per-click (CPC) for some age groups garnered higher percentages than others.

It's always a smart move to begin your Facebook ad campaigns using customer research to ensure that you target the right audience. For example, a leading SEO company called MOZ was able to make one million dollars just because they interviewed their customers the old-fashioned way to understand their needs and thus, improved their product accordingly.

How to Avoid Targeting the wrong Facebook Audience

Do customer research on demographics.

A simple research practice on your customer base to discover the obvious audience demographics, such as job seniority, age, location, education, gender, and even purchasing behavior can tell you a lot. These demographics can be targeted on Facebook. When targeting ads, make sure to remember that you also have to target according to geographic specificity.

Analyze interests—You can also look at Facebook Audience Insights to understand the people who are part of your fanbase Facebook. This tool gives you information that people have expressed on the platform together with the information from reliable third-party apps. When you know the interests of your potential audience, it will become easier to craft relevant messages for your ads and produce a winning ad design.

Target niche interests.

Targeting a wide range of interests instead of focusing on a niche can be detrimental. Best to narrow down your audiences' interests to make it more effective. You can add different layers to the interest so that your audience matches at least one. For example, if you are in the digital education industry, your niches could be: i) digital education resources, ii) teaching resources, iii) online quizzes, iv) interactive games, and v) gamified learning.

2. Low Audience and Offer Match

When crafting your ad messages, you must also consider that not everyone that sees your ad knows your brand. Some audience members are familiar with the benefits of your product but there is a probability that not many ad viewers have heard of your company or brand before. Some of them might ask, "Why am I seeing this ad?"

Your PPC campaign target audience can be summarized into these three different categories:

- People who have never heard of you and have not visited your site.
- People who know who you are but not sure what you do exactly.
- People who have purchased or used your service and product or are at least familiar with your brand, and are on the path of becoming a customer.

Each of the above categories requires a dedicated ad campaign on Facebook so you can hit them in the right spot.

For example, we looked at an ad by a cruise company that wanted to promote a big discount to encourage conversions and attract new customers. The issue here is there was no explanation on what to do with the discount in case someone wanted to use it. The ad makes total sense if the viewer of the ad has interacted with the company before and is aware of its benefits, but to most people, the ad will not make any sense—especially not to any new viewers or users.

A very effective yet simple way that you can evaluate your audience is to check Facebook's Relevance Score, which is a calculated metric that enables marketers and advertisers to understand how an audience reacts to a certain ad.

Adpsresso, when analyzing 104,256 Facebook ads, found that Facebook campaigns' Relevance Score enables marketers to predict both the CPC and click-through rate. Essentially, the higher the ad relevance, the less marketers should pay for conversions and for clicks. You can check your ad's relevance meter when you break down your Facebook reports by performance, as shown in the following image:

3. Targeting Audiences That Are Too Broad

Unless you are a household brand, targeting 20 million people will do more damage than good. Your ad offer, and the copy must be tailored to be relevant to the broader set of people you want to target. You must also be aware where your product stands in the eyes and minds of the general population.

The main issue with targeting a broad range of audience is that your offer may not reach the intended group of people who have the highest purchasing capability due to a limited ad budget. In a sample ad we looked at, the Facebook campaign reached a total of 234,000 people, but the potential size of the audience for all ad groups went over 1.1 million people. What this means is that more than 850,000 people did not see the ad at all because of budget restraints.

How to Tell When your Ad Audience is too Broad?

Your audience size: Ask yourself if the millions of people that reached your ad are really interested in buying your product. If you think the answer is no, it is time to rethink and narrow down your audience to a niche demographic.

Ad reach: This is another way to see if your audience size is too big versus Facebook's projected ad reach and its total audience size. If the campaign shows the budget is for $1,000, then you can reach 150,000 people out of 1 million. You may need to downsize your audience then.

Broad demographics: If you notice that your audience reach is too broad, you can tweak this by excluding certain demographics through using behaviors or interests or even age range and gender.

4. Not Leveraging Custom Audiences

Another big mistake most marketers do is not leveraging their customized audiences. But this is the best way to win with Facebook Ads! Using Facebook custom audiences enables you to reach a target audience that is looking for your products and has the purchasing power as well as the split-second decision-making requirement. Get on Facebook Custom Audiences now to tap into this advertising potential.

How to leverage Facebook Custom Audiences:

Create campaigns to collect leads: You can target previous blog readers and give them an exclusive gift in exchange for their email address. By doing this to a small but committed group of people that is familiar with your brand, they will be much more willing to share their contact details with your business. For this, you need to use the new feature on Facebook called Facebook Leads ads campaign to collect all this information for high-value content of your users.

Remarket to past purchasers: You can also set up Custom Audience based on people who have previously visited your checkout pages or thank you's. This audience can be used for retargeting campaigns for upselling.

5. Not Excluding Past Converters

Most people, when they start out with Facebook advertising, end up making the mistake of forgetting to exclude the audience that has already clicked on an ad and have been converted into a customer. Not excluding past converters may not be an ideal situation because:

- You end up wasting your valuable ad budget resources
- Your ads are not relevant to the people who have been converted.
- The more these people see your ads, the more they'll end up getting annoyed.
- The same people will see your ads over and over again and might suffer from ad fatigue or audience decay.

Facebook Ad Fatigue refers to the same people seeing your ad multiple times a day and their engagement with the ad will likely drop, and that means a higher cost to you, the advertiser.

Facebook Audience Decay refers to you, the advertiser, targeting the same group of people over a time period and diminishing their interest in you simply because they are annoyed with you.

To ensure you exclude these past converters from your Facebook audience, all you need to do is ensure you create a new Custom Audience for the people who have visited your web pages before. Use the "Exclude" feature located in the Audience tab on Facebook when you set up your ad campaign. You can remove the people who have already been to your page at some point.

6. Using the Wrong Ad Type

Using the wrong ad type is one of the most common mistakes. The great thing about Facebook is that advertisers have the freedom to experiment with different types of ads. While the newsfeed ads are one of the easiest and quickest ways to create an ad, that does not mean you should overlook other options such as Video Ads and Leads Ads.

For a quick overview, here are the types of ads on Facebook

you can use:
- Newsfeed Ad.
- Right Column Ad.
- Lead Ads.
- Carousel Ads.
- Dynamic Product Ads / DPA.
- Page Like Ads.
- Canvas Ads.
- Event Ads.
- Mobile App Install Ads.
- GIF Ads.

7. Ads That Fail to Draw Attention

The goal of advertisers is, of course, to create ads that attract. If a niche audience is what you are focusing on, then you need a brilliant ad message that is highly relevant to your target audience. In this day and age, the first thing people look at is images, and then they look at the headline. If your image AND your headline fail to attract the attention of your customers, then the likelihood of them skipping the ad is extremely high.

An ad that fails to attract your audience may be making these mistakes:
- It contains bad photography or low-resolution imaging.
- It does not employ the effective use of colors.
- It contains too many confusing elements that do not match your offer.

Ad research shows that people usually make up their minds within 90 seconds of seeing an ad, and that's a really small window. Research also states that about 63 to 90% of users base their assessment on the colors used on an ad. Adding colorful elements that match your brand will help people notice your ad and also equate it to your brand recognition.

8. Too Much Text on the Ad Image

Back when Facebook got into advertising, the rule was to have only 20% of text, otherwise Facebook could reject your ad. Now, Facebook is not as strict with this ruling, however, your ad ends up fitting into these four categories where Facebook basically rates your ad:

- Okay
- Low
- Medium
- High

You can use various tools like the Text Overlay Tool to test to see if you have too much text.

An ad with high-text density does not mean that Facebook is not going to deliver. However, this really means that you would have a smaller audience that will interact with your ads. Before your ad goes up, Facebook usually notifies you if your ad is text-heavy.

Keep your text density low if you do not want your ad results compromised. You can put in as much text as part of the caption.

9. Headlines without the Right Hook

A study conducted at Columbia University found that 59% of people never read anything more than the headline of your Facebook post before they decide to like it or share it. If you take this information into account, we are usually surrounded by 5,000 ads and branded messages on a daily basis. We are literally immune to ads. Additionally, with today's fast-paced lifestyle, our attention span is quite short. If your headline on your Facebook post fails to catch attention, then people will not read the copy of the ad.

How to write better headlines for your Facebook ads?

- Emphasize the benefits—One of the first things you should do is communicate your product's benefit, and if you can do this in 5 words or less, great! They will be more interested in what you have to offer and want to learn more by reading the copy.
- Keep your ad headlines short and clear—A short post with a 40 character limit was shown to be 86% more effective and received higher engagement than posts with more than 40 characters of words.
- Use numbers in headlines—Numbers attract, and if you use data such as statistics, you are 36% more capable of getting people to click on your ads.

10. Careless Copywriting

Did you know that you can write custom copy for each part of your ad when you create a Facebook ad campaign? A wrong line of text could potentially be the downfall of your ad and push away a reader.

Taking the time to craft high-quality ad copy will take your ad farther. You can also analyze the effectiveness of your campaign by running a split test and experiment with various ad copies.

How to write good Facebook ad copy:
- Begin by defining your goal for your ad. What is your ad campaign goal? To get people to buy something? To collect new leads? To create brand awareness? Each of the sentences you put in your ad should point towards your goal and nudge the audience to do what the ad says.
- Find the right tone of voice.
- Stick to what's important.
- Write with the customer in mind.

Testimonials are also a great way to write an ad copy. Research conducted by Econsultancy says that a website using customer reviews often get, at least, an increase of 63% of visitors who end up buying something.

Avoid putting in any cryptic or vague copy as people might not understand what you are trying to say. Keep your copy trustworthy, informative, and clear.

11. Missing a Clear Value Offer

Value offer is literally your goals translated into a focal point that you know will entice your customers. If the goal of your advertisement is to represent the key actions that your audience would most likely need to make, then the value offer should explain why they should take those specific steps.

You should also make sure your UVP (Unique Value Proposition) is clear, and it describes your product's benefit while differentiating you from the competition.

Essentially, you want to follow these rules for positioning your UVP: Your UVP should be in the customer's language. Do not let them guess.

- UVPs should be clear and easy to comprehend.
- UVP should be different and better than the competitors.
- Avoid hype words. People don't buy that anymore.
- UVP should be easy to read and understood in 5 seconds or less.

If you have these things down, you are in for a stellar ad! You should also remember to place your UVP in the headline, or front and center of your ad's image as this is the most visible location. Your ad message is delivered at first sight.

12. Stuffing Ads with Too Much Text

When it comes to Facebook ads, less is often more. The fewer distractions you have on your ad copy, the better since it gets your message across and helps people convert easily. On average, Facebook page posts usually are in the region of 157.7 characters, while user posts generate 121.5 characters and mobile posts, even less with 104.9 characters. Posts which a character range of 140 to 159 are usually 13.3% less engaging, on average, compared to posts with 120 to 139 characters.

One of the reasons why shorter Facebook posts work is because they are more concise, and they deliver the UVP message quickly. If you are creating a blog article, then a longer introductory ad will definitely make more sense.

13. Forgetting to Caption Video Ads

We tend to forget certain things about human nature. It is the same with Facebook video ads. Oftentimes, we forget that we need to add captions for the video, because by default videos are muted in the newsfeed. Facebook says that captioned video ads increase viewership by 12% on average. In another study, it showed that 41% of videos were completely ineffective without sound.

The chances of people not clicking "play" if you do not caption your video ads are high. This is due to the fact that they will not be able to see your ad or know what it is about.

Here are other things you want to avoid with video ad engagements:
- Not including an intro.
- Putting logos or credits at the beginning of the video.
- Attempting to put too much information in a single video.
- Using a person to speak on camera without sufficient context.

Making a video can take several days or, at the very least, several hours. Having a storyboard and thinking it through before starting the project is a best practice.

14. Bad Choice of Ad Placement

Score marketers found that desktop Facebook ads have a higher cost-per-click of 534% more than ads placed on an audience network + mobile. Desktop ads also perform much better in conversions. The ad placement plays a crucial role in the results of an ad. Facebook's ad placements include:

- Facebook newsfeeds (mobile and desktop).
- Right-hand column Facebook.
- Instagram.
- Audience Network.
- Instant Articles.
- In-stream Video.

Another reason why marketers make the mistake in choosing ad placements is the offer as well as the placement mismatch. For instance, if your goal is to create free trials for your software, Instagram ads may not be the best option because people are less likely to deal with businesses when they browse images of their friends.

One good way to find out if the ad placement brings in high returns on your investment is to do multiple ad placements and then analyze the results.

You can break down reports using Facebook Ads Manager and analyze which ads have lower cost-per-click and the highest conversion rate.

In case you are not sure which ad placements you should begin with, here are some suggestions:

- Conversions: Facebook and Audience Network.
- Brand awareness: Facebook and Instagram.

- Video views: Facebook, Instagram, and Audience Network.
- App installs: Facebook, Instagram, and Audience Network.
- Traffic (for website clicks and app engagement): Facebook and Audience Network
- Product catalog sales: Facebook and Audience Network.
- Engagement: Facebook and Instagram.

15. The 24/7 Ad Delivery

Having your ads run on a schedule makes more sense than having it run all day, all night. Here are some reasons why running ads all the time does not make sense:

- Audiences get tired of seeing your ad more quickly
- Your budget is spent on low-traffic hours when the conversion is very little.

To prevent ad fatigue and to ensure that you have your ad frequency under control, you can set up a custom schedule and promote your ads for a specific duration and time during the entire week. If you are worried that Facebook might end up delivering your ads to the same audience too many times per day, then you can also cap this using the Daily Unique Reach.

16. Amateur Ad Bidding

When it comes to ads, Facebook functions on an auction-type bidding feature the same way Google AdWords works. This is called PPC bidding, and it works extremely well when the stage is set just right. You can view and customize your bidding through Facebook Ads Manager using the "Budget and Schedule" tab.

Facebook ads have four different bidding options:

- *Conversions*–Your ads will be delivered as optimally as possible by Facebook to people who are most likely to convert. This method is a great area to start as Facebook optimizes the ad for you.
- *Link Clicks*–Facebook's primary goal is getting users to click on your ad and to follow the link or whichever goal you determine, whether it's to go to your websites landing page or view your Facebook profile.
- *Impressions*–Your ad is optimized with the main objective of increasing visibility to as many people as possible. This is a good option for businesses looking to build and strengthen brand awareness or sharing highly engaging content.
- *Daily Unique Reach*–Facebook optimizes increasing the visibility of your ads to people once a day. This is an excellent retargeting method to ensure that people will see your ads at least once every day and may not get tired or annoyed quickly.

There are three elements that determine your ad cost. These are: your ad relevance; your bid; and action rates, determined by Facebook algorithms. There is no right or wrong bidding method for any particular ad type. You just find the best bidding methods based on what's good and what works for your brand.

17. Slow Campaign Take-Off

A slow campaign take-off could be due to many reasons, some of them could be:

- There are just too many ad groups with A/B test variations with low budgets.
- The images used in the ad are not good enough to attract people's attention.
- The low relevance of ads due to poor audience targeting.
- Using the wrong bidding options.
- Being impatient and making unnecessary changes.
- Too much text.

So, what is the solution?

When starting a new campaign, you can assign Lifetime budgets that cross your planned budget. You are looking at about 10,000 impressions to check which ads work and which don't.

Use Facebook as a resource for the start of the campaign. For example, hit your campaign running with a budget of $1,500 instead of the planned $300, just to get the ball rolling.

18. Leaving Facebook No Time for Optimization

Another common rookie mistake with Facebook ads is to rely too much on immediate gratification and expecting Facebook to deliver astounding results in just a few hours. Don't write off a campaign as a failure if just after 3 hours, you don't see results. Usually, it takes about 24 hours for Facebook to optimize campaigns and a full 48 hours to reach a potential audience and bring in the results you want. Each time you make substantial changes to your campaign, wait

24 to 48 hours to expect any results or draw any conclusions.

19. Guessing, Not Testing

Another rookie mistake is not testing your ads but only guessing which works best. One of the best things you can do for the effort you put into creating your ads is running an A/B test to see which image ad performs best.

Doing a test enables you to have different options for images and ads rather than just relying on one. When you are not sure of your target audience or which ad copy to use or even what ad image works best, always experiment with the options you have.

20. Doing the Wrong Kind of A/B Tests

While testing is essential, conducting the wrong test is also a waste of time. Not every split testing you do is a brilliant idea. Your A/B testing is restricted to just a few tests a month on average due to limited ad budgets. A program called Optimizely has crafted a chart to assist experienced and less experienced A/B testers to prioritize tests efficiently.

A/B test elements that provide the biggest results:
- Countries.
- Precise interests.
- Mobile OS.
- Age ranges.
- Genders.
- Ad images.
- Titles.
- Relationship status.

- Landing page.
- Interested in.

There are plenty of different elements that connect to your target audience, which tell you how extremely important it is to figure out who to target, how often, how much, and so on.

21. Testing Too Many Things at Once

Sometimes, it is also easy for marketers and advertisers to get caught up in using different A/B testing simply because we want to see results in different situations. Plenty of people take research from step one and collect and lump all their interests into a huge list on Facebook Ad Manager, hoping to reach a large segment of the market. This is no doubt a bad practice as it will cost marketers much more money than their expenditure in the ad. You will get results, but you will not know which audience interest brought in the appropriate results.

This is like putting all your eggs in one basket and hoping for the biggest and best results.

For every experiment that you run, you will need to make sure that there is enough data for the testing results to show clear, valid, and statistically significant data. You should aim to collect at least 500 conversions before any conclusions are drawn. If there are two variations tested, then you need more ad impressions as well as conversions to pinpoint on a winning formula.

22. Low Landing Page and Facebook Ad Match

Imagine clicking on an ad for bar soap but being directed to a site where they sell portable chargers. That would be confusing and will only make the user have less trust towards the brand. Unfortunately, some marketers do not see this as a problem, and that's why users see plenty of Facebook ads that lead to irrelevant pages.

Promising one thing but delivering another thing, plus failing to retain a consistent message throughout your sales channel, is a costly and grave mistake.

When a user is interested in a specific product and clicks on an ad only to land on a different landing page, they will feel misled, lose interest, and leave the page. To maintain your landing page's value propositions and to keep your Facebook ad aligned, you must use the same key messages that are consistent throughout your sales funnel.

You should also avoid targeting all kinds of potential users in one go. Address your audience by segmenting them and connecting them with niche ad campaigns.

23. Poor Landing Page UX

Certain mistakes on your website's landing page will make you lose conversions. Even if your Facebook ad is amazing, landing page issues could compromise the effectiveness of your Facebook ads. Where Facebook ads are concerned, you should remember ad placements when you construct your landing page.

For example, if the mobile audience is what you are targeting, then make sure your landing page is optimized for mobile users and not desktop users. Crafting responsive designs to suit mobile users or desktop users should correlate with what your brand is giving as well as where your users usually hang-out. That said, almost 80% of users access websites through mobile anyway, and that's where most revenue also comes from. It is now more important to keep your landing page mobile optimized than ever before.

24. Neglecting the Conversion Tracking

It is extremely tempting to do conversion tracking and get your Facebook campaigns up and running. However, not tracking your conversions is not a sustainable route. Not conducting tracking means that you are doing your ads blindly. There is no way to analyze your ad results.

While you can see rudimentary trackings such as click-through rates and other metrics without doing any tracking adjustments, you do not have tracking for off-site conversions. Facebook can track off-platform conversions using Facebook Pixel. You just need to make sure to install it on your website.

To set up the basic Facebook Pixel code, follow these guidelines:

1. Go to the Pixels Page in Ads Manager.

2. Click Actions > View Code.

Each Facebook Ad Manager account can only have a one-pixel code. Use this pixel code on each page of your website.

3. Copy the code and paste it between the <head> tags on each web page, or in your website template to install it on your entire website. You can also use **Google Tag Manager**. To track specific conversions such as lead conversions or even purchases, you need to add a conversion tracking code. What's great is that you can track nine different specific events with Facebook Pixel:

This is a must-have in tracking your Facebook ad conversion, especially if you want to discover new advertising possibilities as well as establish successful A/B testing.

25. Losing Sight of the Real Goal

Each time you log into Facebook ads, be wary of vanity metrics such as your click-through rates and your cost-per-clicks. None of that matters if that data does not contribute to the ultimate goal you've established; whether that is increasing sales, increasing website visits, or increasing brand awareness or anything else. While the vanity metrics are great to look at, do not lose sight of your main goals when you analyze your campaign results.

26. Leaving Ads Unattended

Ads need to be tweaked, reviewed, and edited if necessary. Treat them like pets. Once you leave them alone, your ads could behave badly. AdEspresso had a first-hand lesson on this issue. They set up incredibly well-crafted and well-performing ad campaigns and left the campaigns to run for several months.

During that five month period, the cost-per-conversion on average for their campaigns increased by 1050%, going from $3.33 to $38.47. They threw in plenty of money but reached a relatively small audience and were saturated in just two months. To ensure that your Facebook ad campaigns remain under control, you must check up on them weekly. You will be better off reviewing ad campaigns more often than not once you have done the initial setup.

Here are the eight Facebook Ad metrics you need to keep track of:
- Ad frequency.
- Relevance score.
- Click-through-rate vs. conversion rate.
- Number of leads.
- Facebook Ads customer churn.
- Ad performance by placement.
- Clicks by interests.
- Ad engagement rate.

27. Neglecting the Ad Frequency

Ad frequency shows you how many times a person has seen

your ad on an average basis. The higher your ad frequency, the higher the likelihood that people will become tired and bored seeing your ad multiple times. AdEspresso also analyzed how frequency affects the click-through rate, cost-per-click, and cost-per-conversion of ad campaigns. Here are their findings:

Frequency	CTR Decrease	CPC Increase
1	0	0
2	-8.91%	+49.82%
3	-16.92%	+62.20%
4	-23.34%	+68.02%
5	-29.72%	+98.51%
6	-41.19%	+127.32%
7	-41.38%	+127.26%
8	-48.97%	+138.31%
9	-49.87%	+161.15%

Source: *https://adespresso.com/blog/facebook-ads-frequency/*

The click-through-rate decreased as much as 8.91% when the same people saw the ad twice. However, when shown repetitive ads for 5 consecutive times, the cost-per-click increased to 98.51% higher compared to the first ad delivery.

The general rule is to keep your ad frequency to 3-5 points, unless your ad is really entertaining and has become viral.

Remarketing of Facebook campaigns have shown better results even when the ad frequency was over 10 ad views. Never make the rookie mistake of neglecting ad frequencies that are high since you can use it as an indicator your campaigns may need updated.

28. Not Using Auto-Optimization

If you are worried about high ad frequency and decreasing

campaign results, and you're also spending too much time checking your ad reports on Facebook, you can efficiently tackle this task through Facebook Automated Rules. This feature enables marketers to keep ad campaigns under control.

It also allows four things to take place automatically. You can:
- Turn off (campaign, ad set or ad).
- Send notification to the ad manager (you).
- Adjust budget (increase/decrease daily/lifetime budget by…).
- Adjust manual bid (increase/decrease bid by…).

These rules can be applied to any specific campaign, ad sets, and ads that you have selected. You can also use it on active campaigns.

The current conditions you can set are:
- Cost per Result.
- Cost per Add Payment Info (Facebook Pixel).
- Cost per Click (Link).
- Cost per App Install.
- Cost per Add to Cart (Facebook Pixel).
- Cost per Initiate Checkout (Facebook Pixel).
- Cost per Purchase (Facebook Pixel).
- Cost per Lead (Facebook Pixel).
- Cost per Complete Registration (Facebook Pixel).
- CPM (Cost per 1,000 impressions).
- Daily Spent.
- Frequency.
- Impressions.
- Lifetime Spent.
- Reach.
- Results.

If you want to create a new ad rule, all you do is select one or various campaigns or ads, and then click on Create Rule.

Once you have selected the campaign or ad, you can then create custom combinations or specific conditions that may trigger specific actions.

For instance, you can check to see if Facebook can automatically turn off active ads in your campaign with an ad frequency of more than 4.

This automated rule feature does a good job of notifying a marketer when a campaign begins to garner lower results, and it also helps to keep ad costs under control.

29. Missing Out on the Conclusions

There are some marketers who have run multiple Facebook ad campaigns but always end up making the same mistakes. You can avoid this by keeping a log of your ad campaigns or tracking the results in an excel spreadsheet.

In a spreadsheet you can note key achievements, takeaways, and any mistakes you've made for each Facebook campaign.

Take a few minutes to conclude what you have done in your previous Facebook campaign before you trash it; take note of what worked and what went wrong. It is always a good idea to double down on what works.

Chapter 7: Understanding Facebook Advertising

To understand Facebook advertising is to know what Facebook Business Manager is. The Facebook Business Manager tool is designed for managing your Facebook pages and ad accounts.

When you use this, you will be able to:

- Manage your Facebook page admins and ad accounts.
- see who has access to your pages and ad accounts.
- remove or change admin permissions.
- work with agencies and also share your business account with agencies, so they can manage your ad campaigns via Facebook.
- Manage multiple ad accounts as well as users all under the Business Manager account.

Essentially, there are two main roles in the Facebook Business Manager, which are the Admin and Employee.

Each of these roles have different access levels. There is also a different tool for Facebook ad accounts that enables the admin to manage and edit in the business account itself.

To start advertising on Facebook, you will be required to have a Business Manager account that enables you to manage at least one Facebook Page.

To add an advertising account to your Business Manager:

- Open your Business Manager Settings.
- Under the tab People and Assets, click on "Ad Accounts."
- On the right side of the page, select "Add New Ad Accounts."

- Choose one of the 3 options: "Claim Ad Account," "Request Access to an Ad Account," or "Create a New Ad Account."

You also need to add a credit card to the account and provide other essential information before advertising.

Setting Up Your Ad Account Info

Facebook will not allow you to start spending unless there is a value payment connected and some relevant business information shared. To set up your account, click on "Ad Account Settings" on your Business Manager.

Fill in the necessary information for your business, such as the address.

Billing details can be added under the "Payments" tab by clicking on "Add Payment Method." Some localities request VAT numbers. You can also choose the currency you want to deal with and your specific time zone. Once you have filled in your account information, click on "Save Changes." You can then proceed to the "Billing & Payment Methods" page.

Setting Up Your Billing & Payment Information

Adding credit card details should be done under "Billing & Payment Methods" in the Business Manager menu.

At the Billing section, you can do the following:
- Insert new payment methods.
- Edit your existing payment methods.
- Set the spending limit for your account.

If you would like to add a new payment method:
- Click on "Add Payment Method."

- Choose the method you want to add.
- Fill in the specific information.
- Click on "Continue."

Multiple payment types are accepted by Facebook; the major ones being credit cards and PayPal payments.

As you begin adding more advertising content, it would be good practice to add a secondary payment option. Should your primary card expire or if you reach your monthly limit, or worse it is blocked for some reason, your campaigns can still run with a secondary payment option. If Facebook does not have enough funds, your campaigns could be paused until you top up the necessary funds, and you could end up having to restart them one by one manually. Facebook will automatically bill your secondary credit card when your primary card is unavailable. This keeps things running smoothly.

Editing Your Payment Options

Should you want to make changes to your Facebook advertising payments, you can do it via the same page by clicking on "Edit Payment Methods."

You will not be able to delete your primary source of payment unless you add another payment method. Only then can you delete your primary option. This works for most payment options on the net.

How and when are you billed? Billing is often done on two occasions:

- At the end of every month.

- When you reach your billing limit.

Billing limit or threshold is what you will be billed on your primary payment method each time you reach a limit. The amount of this limit is based on your billing history, and it usually varies.

When you first start advertising, this threshold is usually low at around $25. Each time you spend $25, you will be billed for that same amount. However, as you continue spending and your payments are processed correctly, your threshold is automatically increased to anywhere from $50, $250, $500, and finally, $750.

These limits don't have any immediate impact on your advertising campaigns. They just affect how often you will be charged.

Dealing with fewer invoices is the advantage to having a higher threshold.

You can always contact Facebook should you have any issues with billing or if you want to change your threshold.

Setting up the Account Spending Limit

You can cap your account spending if you do not want your ad campaigns to exceed your advertising budget. This is also important when you have given agencies access to your ad manager account and want to only spend what has been budgeted.

Setting the limit is very simple. Just click the "Set Account Spending Limit" and set the amount. Do not set it too low or you will end up updating your limit often. Each time your limit is reached, your account(s) will be paused for at least 15 minutes. It should also be noted: your account spending limit does not have an impact on your ad's delivery pace.

Facebook Ad Account Limits

Limits, unfortunately, exist in Facebook Ads but these limits are not a hindrance to your campaigns. While it's not bothersome, it is still good to know what these limits are.

Here are the limits of Facebook Power Editor:

- Users can manage up to a maximum of 25 ad accounts.

- Each ad account can contain up to 25 users.

- An average ad account contains approximately 5,000 ads and 1,000 ad sets.

These limits apply to ads and campaigns that have not been deleted. Even when you reach your limit, you can always delete older campaigns and their ads.

Review Your Notification Settings

Obviously, you will want to stay informed regarding any updates occurring on your ad account. Make sure you turn on your Facebook Notifications, so you know what is happening with your campaigns. Sometimes, they can flood your inbox.

You may want to do one of two things:

1. Change the frequency of the email notifications.

2. Separate your email from Facebook so it goes into a different tab or folder and not in your primary inbox.

To edit your notification settings:

- Click on the settings tab on the Ad Account Page.

- Click on "Notifications" from the menu on the left.

- You can add or remove notifications, based on what you want to be notified about.

- You can set up notifications, so you receive the most important ones.

Review Your Ad Account Roles

If adding new user admins is what you want to do with your Facebook advertising account, then click on "Account Roles."

In this section, you can add new admins or edit permissions for existing users.

Once you are done with this, you have set up your account management, and you are all set!

Traffic and Leads for Your Website

The most common use for Facebook Ads is to drive traffic to a specific website and also to create brand awareness. Directing users to your site can increase the website's overall reach, get users to buy your product, sign up for your service, or subscribe to your newsletter.

Various types of ads and how you can use them to drive traffic to your site:

Link Click Ads

Supported placements:

- Column Desktop.

- Newsfeed Mobile.

- Newsfeed Audience.

- Network Instagram.

Specs:

- Recommended image size: 1,200 x 628 pixels.

- Ad copy text: 90 characters.

- Headline: 25 characters.

- Link Description: 30 characters.

When you think Facebook ads, the first thing that might come to mind is Link Click Ads. This ad serves to promote external websites and also send users to a specific landing page or even a specific blog post. Link Click Ads can be used with several placements, which enables marketers to provide the same ad across various newsfeeds and effectively reach a large audience. This type of ad performs exceptionally well and can also generate likes for your page, but don't forget to check the comments you receive and reply to them because this contributes to the ad's performance and engagement.

Video Ads

Supported placements:
- Newsfeed Mobile.

- Newsfeed Audience.

- Network Instagram.

This is another form of Link Click Ads, but instead of a stationary image, you use a video.

Specs:
- Ad copy text: 90 characters.

- Aspect ratios supported: 16:9 to 9:16.

- File size: up to 4 GB max.

- Continuous looping available.

- Video can be as long as 120 minutes, but most top-performing videos are 15-30 seconds.

Boosted Page Posts

Supported placements:
- Newsfeed Mobile.

- Newsfeed Audience.

- Network Instagram.

Each time you post on your page, Facebook gives you a chance to boost your post. You will see a conveniently located button at the bottom right corner of a post. When you click on it, you can set the post to target a specific audience, add in your bidding methods, as well as promote your page's post to more people on Facebook.

Specs:

- Recommended image size: 1,200 x 628 pixels.

- Ad copy text: unlimited.

- Headline: 25 characters.

- Link Description: 30 characters.

The Boosted Page Post will look exactly like any other Facebook post, except "Sponsored" will appear at the top of the ad.

Multi-Product (Carousel Ads)

Supported placements:
- Newsfeed Mobile.

- Newsfeed Audience.

- Network Instagram.

This carousel format allows the advertiser to add up to 10 items, which could be a combination of videos and images and even links to a single ad unit.

For e-commerce advertisers looking to promote a variety of products from their store, this is an extremely convenient and useful feature.

This feature really works great even for marketers wanting to promote different types of posts and offers, and it attracts audiences to view a variety of content based on the brand or product.

Specs:

- Recommended image size: 1080 x 1080 or 600 x 600 pixels.

- Ad copy text: 90 characters.

- Headline: 25 characters.

- Link Description: 30 characters.

Dynamic Product Ads (DPA)

Supported placements:

- Newsfeed Mobile.

- Newsfeed Right Column.

- Audience Network.

- Instagram.

These dynamic product ads that Facebook has introduced are like remarketing display ads on speed. These ads target users based on previous actions whether on your website or application with an ad that is perfectly timed.

To use this feature, all you need to do is upload your product catalog and double check that your Facebook pixel is installed on all your site pages. This means Facebook handles the retargeting and automation for you.

Specs:

- Recommended image size: 1,200 x 628 pixels or 600 x 600 pixels.

- Ad copy text: 90 characters.

- Headline: 25 characters.

- Link Description: 30 characters.

Facebook Lead Ads

Supported placements:

- Newsfeed Mobile.

- Newsfeed Audience.

- Network Instagram.

Lead Ads are one of the best ways to get leads. This type of ad allows users to download your content or sign up for an offer without ever leaving Facebook's platform. Lead Ads are perfect for attaining potential customers email address.

Specs:

- Recommended image size: 1,200 x 628 pixels.

- Ad copy text: 90 characters.

- Headline: 25 characters.

- Link Description: 30 characters.

Context card can be in paragraph format, which has no character limit, or 5-bullet point format, which allows for 80 characters per bullet.

- Context card headline: 60 characters.

- Context card button: 30 characters.

- Privacy Policy and website URL links are required.

The moment someone has filled in the form, Facebook ad accounts stores the email address. Among the easiest ways to transfer new leads from Facebook to your CRM system is to automate the whole process. This is one extra thing you can do when setting up as campaigns via Facebook.

Canvas Ads

Supported placements:
- Mobile Newsfeed.

Canvas by Facebook is completely interactive and allows users to engage with your brand on Facebook; it is only available on mobile version as it was built for mobile usage. Using Canvas enables your audience to swipe through a carousel of images, and even tilt it in different directions. You can zoom in and zoom out using your fingertips. Canvas loads much faster than average mobile web apps.

Specs:
- Recommended image size: 1,200 x 628 pixels.
- Ad copy text: 90 characters.
- Headline: 45 characters.

Canvas has the following possible components:
- Header with logo.
- Full-screen image.
- Text block.
- Button for offsite links.
- Image carousel.
- Auto-play video.
- Full-screen tilt-to-pan image.
- Product set.

Collection Ads

Supported placements:
- Mobile Newsfeed.

With Collection Ads, you can showcase several products sold on your site on Facebook. This new format enables people to discover your brand, browse your products, and purchase your products in a highly visual and immersive channel.

Specs:

- Image Size: 1,200 x 628 pixels recommended.

- Image Ratio: 1.9:1.

- Headline: 25 characters recommended

Like & Engagement for Your Page

The type of ad you choose on Facebook depends entirely on the campaign outcome you are looking for. Two particular campaign objectives help to increase the number of likes on your Facebook page as well as increase the reach of your content posted. With recent updates to Facebook, your regular posts on your page will reach an organic audience of 2-3%. Using Facebook ads is a great way to let all your fans and potential fans see your messages.

Page Like Ads

Supported placements:

- Column Desktop.

- Newsfeed Mobile.

- Newsfeed.

Page Like Ads are the most commonly used ads to increase page Likes. These ads can be displayed on a variety of placements and also include a visible call-to-action for users to like your page immediately. When you advertise for likes, keep in mind that it's not about getting any random person to like your page. It is about choosing the right audience interested in your page and the content it offers. To achieve increased likes, it is important to pick the right image, so you maximize the performance of Facebook ads and improve reach.

Page Post Photo Ads

Supported placements:
- Column Desktop.
- Newsfeed Mobile.
- Newsfeed.

When should you engage your page's fans? Using the page photo ads is the best time to feature beautiful images. Choose the right image, and set yourself up with comments, likes, and increased interaction. You can also insert specific links in your text description, so people can be directed to a page on your website.

Page Post Video Ads

Supported placements:
- Column Desktop.
- Newsfeed Mobile.
- Newsfeed.

One of the highest engagement procurers is Video Advertising. It creates a strong connection between brand and user, and almost any company can make simple videos to connect with their audience and speak to them in the way images cannot.

Video ads also have the ability to retarget a certain segment of visitors based on how much of the video they have watched. Because of this, video ads are perfect for retargeting especially with other types of ads.

Specs:

- Ad copy text: 90 characters.

- Aspect Ratios Supported: 16:9 (full landscape) to 9:16 (full portrait).

- File size: up to 4 GB max.

- Video can be as long as 120 minutes, but most top-performing videos are 15-30 seconds.

- Audio: Stereo AAC audio compression, 128kbps + preferred.

Page Post Text

Supported placements:
- Column Desktop.

- Newsfeed Mobile.

- Newsfeed.

This ad format is focused on page engagement. Despite that, not many marketers use it when there is the photo option. In truth, pictures perform better for most audiences. Avoid this ad if you can unless you have a stellar tagline that will bring in the audience that you want.

Mobile and Desktop Apps Install

Facebook has become the biggest mobile advertiser since the launch of its mobile application. The App Install offers a distinctive opportunity to attract all mobile users on iOS and Android. These ad extensions are useful and should be taken into account if you are in the mobile app industry, especially since they are built for that specific purpose.

Mobile App

Supported placements:
- Mobile Newsfeed.

Using the Mobile App Ads is a perfect choice if you want to drive mobile app installations. Ads are displayed and optimized for the mobile version of Facebook's newsfeed. When users click on install as a call-to-action, they will be directed immediately to the App Store pop up. This definitely increases conversion rates. There will be plenty more targeting options when using Facebook's mobile ad format. For instance, when you choose the iOS/Android version, you are targeting users on tablets and mobile devices. You could also target only users connected to a Wi-Fi network.

Specs:
- Recommended image size: 1,200 x 628 pixels.

- Image ratio: 1.9:1.

- Ad copy text: Up to 90 characters.

- Your image may not include more than 20% text.

Desktop App

Supported placements:
- Column Desktop.

- Newsfeed.

Enables you to channel users to your Facebook wall and engage with it.

Specs:

- Recommended image size: 1,200 x 628 pixels.

- Image ratio: 1.9:1.

- Ad copy text: Up to 90 characters.

Instagram Mobile App Ads

Supported placements: Instagram

You can also advertise your mobile app via Instagram. This is perfect since Instagram is only useable on mobile, which means users who access your ad are interested in what you have to offer and are more likely to download your app. Both video ads and photo ads work in Instagram Mobile App Ads.

Specs:

- Image ratio: 1:1.

- Image size: 1080 x 1080 pixels.

- Minimum resolution: 600 x 315 pixels / 600 x 600 pixels / 600 x 750 pixels.

- Maximum resolution: 1936 x 1936 pixels.

- Caption: Text only, 125 characters recommended.

- Visitors to Your Store or Event.

When targeted effectively, these ads perform very well.

Event Ads

Supported placements:
- Right Column.

- Desktop Newsfeed.

- Mobile Newsfeed.

Facebook Events, while not exactly a form of advertising, is an exceptional way to attract online attendees. Using Facebook events can dramatically boost your event coverage, especially when the right kind of targeting is used.

Based on the relevance and size of your event, limiting your geographical reach will help in attracting a niche living in the same region or city as the event.

Specs:
- Recommended image size: 1920×1080 pixels.

- Image ratio: 1.9:1.

- Ad copy text: Up to 90 characters.

- Headline: 25 characters.

- Link Description: 30 characters.

- Offer Claims.

- Supported placements: Right.

- Column Desktop.

- Newsfeed.

- Mobile Newsfeed.

This feature is ideal for any physical store owner who wants to attract people to their store, especially for sales or any seasonal promotion. Once your offer ad is live, an interested user who clicks on your ad and redeems the offer will subsequently receive an email containing the details and terms of use.

Specs:

- Recommended image size: 1,200 x 628 pixels.

- Image ratio: 1.9:1.

- Offer title: Up to 25 characters.

- Ad copy text: Up to 90 characters.

To be able to craft an offer, your page should have garnered at least 50 likes.

Local Awareness Ads

Supported placements:

- Column Desktop.

- Newsfeed.

- Mobile Newsfeed.

Using Local Awareness Ads is another excellent way to garner attention to your store. This ad type works well combined with Facebook's location-based targeting, helping you to reach people who are currently near your store. There are different call-to-actions which you can use such as "Call Now," and "Send Message." People can easily and conveniently contact or find you.

Specs:

- Recommended image size: 1,200 x 628 pixels.

- Image ratio: 1.9:1.

- Text: 90 characters.

- Headline: 25 characters.

- News Feed description: 30 characters.

Who are your customers?

Getting to know your customers is an integral part of successful Facebook ad campaigns. With over 1 billion active users daily, it is crucial that you target specific audiences truly interested in your product.

Advertising is getting the right customers and not about getting random clicks or likes. You want to choose the audience that sees the benefits of your product, but you should also keep testing your options to see which one works in what condition and what platform.

How to Create Facebook Audiences

You need to use this convenient Facebook tool called "Audience Manager Tool" to create niche audiences and manage these different categories. This tool is found in the Business Manager application at the Audiences Tab.

At this tab, you can see all the Facebook audiences you have created and saved. To understand targeting possibilities, let's look at the primary audience types that Facebook has:

- Saved Audiences.

- Custom Audiences.

- Lookalike Audiences.

These various types of audiences provide plenty of additional options for crafting the perfect target audience for your Facebook campaigns.

Facebook Saved Audiences

Saved audiences are the variety that can be defined by choosing people's age, gender, interests, income level, and even devices. Saved audiences can be created in the campaign setup phase or in the Audience Manager.

Location-based targeting

Facebook also allows you to target people in specific locations, including:

- Country.
- State/Region.
- Counties.
- DMA (Designated Market Area).
- City.
- Postal Code.
- Specific Address Radius.

All you need to do is type in the area or region you want to target.

Another layer of location targeting you can do to make it more specific is to locate using the last updated location of an actual Facebook user.

- People who live in this location—Location is determined by the location on a user's Facebook profile and confirmed by their IP address.
- People recently in this location—use data in the mobile device usage in the geographic area you intend to target.
- People traveling to this location—Users who keyed in a specific geographic area as a recent location that is, at least, 100 miles away from their home location.

Demographics-based targeting

When you click on the Demographics tab, you will find even more targeting topics to refine your audience based on many options.

The basic 3 are:

- Age–if you want to target audiences based on a specific age group, you can easily refine it by providing Facebook what your ideal customer's age range is.
- Gender–You can also target a particular gender that would appeal to your brand
- Language–Target the people who can understand your ads in a specific language.

There are more refined categories if you want to be more specific, such as political views, life events, job titles, ethnicity, and so on.

Interest-based targeting

The best and easiest Facebook ad targeting options is "Interests" because they allow you to pinpoint on people specifically interested in a subject related to your product. You could target people interested in your competitor or your broader market segment, or even specific magazines and blogs related to your industry.

To create targeting based on interests, you can simply type in one interest or browse the selection with hundreds of interests, and Facebook will suggest other related topics.

These interests are calculated on a user's behavior on Facebook, their likes and interests, apps they have engaged in, pages they have liked, and more. Adding more than one interest will specifically target people with, at least, one of them, which will make your reach broader.

Behavior-based targeting

Behaviors are different from "Interests" in a way that it is focused on the user's purchasing history, events they like, personal anniversaries, etc. This data is collected by Facebook by analyzing various data sets; external and internal. While they are not always mandatory, they work great for targeting people who have recently purchased something; such as planning a holiday or preparing for one.

This information can be extremely useful if you are in the hotel industry or traveling industry. It is worth checking to see if they can work for your business.

Facebook Custom Audiences

These types of target audiences are perhaps your highest value as they enable you to retarget past website visitors as well as users who have previously engaged with your content. There are plenty of ways to create custom audiences.

Creating Custom Audiences from Customer Files

You can create your Facebook Custom Audience by checking your existing customer files and look at email accounts, phone numbers, location, and even app IDs. This information is helpful in targeting newsletter subscribers as well as app users.

Here are the steps to create a custom audience:
- Create a Facebook Custom Audience.
- Choose the "Customer File" option.
- Choose either to add a customer file or import contacts from MailChimp.
- Import your customer data to create a new Custom Audience.
- Select your identifiers.

- Upload a customer file.
- Give your Custom Audience a name.
- Customer files can include 15 different identifiers, the most popular ones being:
- Email.
- Phone number.
- Mobile advertiser ID.

Creating Custom Audiences Based on Website Traffic

Website traffic allows you to create re-marketing and retargeting campaigns for people who have previously engaged with your app or website. This traffic is always very high value as these users who are seeing your ad now have already shown a degree of interest in your product previously. If your website is built on a WordPress platform, you can create custom audiences using the Pixel Caffeine plugin.

You also need to have the Facebook Pixel installed. Next, just go to the Audience Manager and create your Custom Audience based on your previous website traffic history.

Here, you have multiple options of targeting to choose from:
- You can choose to target people who have visited your website.
- You can choose to target people who have visited specific websites related to your industry.
- You can choose people who have visited specific web pages.
- You can choose to target people who have not visited your website for a period of time.
- A combination of the choices above.

Creating Custom Audiences Based on App Activity

You can also reach out to users who have engaged with your app and set up a specific Facebook audience for those types of groups. To do this, you can target users based on their app activity, but first you also need to register your app and set it up in the **app events**. You can now target people who have made specific actions on your app and even target them based on a specific timeframe.

For instance, you can select an activity based on a purchasing event and specify, "In the Last 90 days" to reach people who have completed an in-app purchase event in the past 90 days.

Creating Custom Audiences Based on Engagement

Another way you can target specific users is to look at how they have engaged with your Facebook content such as the videos they have seen or the posts they have liked on your Page.

Custom Audiences has the capacity to focus on people who have conducted the following activity:
- Visited your Facebook Page.
- Engaged with your Facebook Page posts or ads.
- Clicked on any call-to-action buttons.
- Sent a message to your Page.
- Saved your Page or posts.

This targeting option enables you to reach a "high-potential" audience since they are most likely interested in learning about what you have to offer.

How to Narrow Down Your Audiences

Narrowing your audience is the same as niche targeting. You want to focus on users that have the highest potential of engagement and who make purchasing decision to purchase your product or service or attend your event or engage in your activity. It doesn't matter if you have a huge advertising budget. Targeting and narrowing down your audience ensures you meet the right ones without wasting your time.

You can narrow your audience pool with targeting options when you create your Saved Audiences, by adding or subtracting different targeting options based on your specific marketing needs. In doing so, your audience pool will either grow bigger or smaller. This will ultimately help you create niche audiences.

You can include or exclude your interests or demographics, so your ads reach the relevant people and not the same people over and over.

Facebook Ads Reporting & Optimization

When you are done setting up your Facebook Ad Campaign, whether it is your first or your twentieth, you still need to continue monitoring and reviewing your campaigns, even though Facebook does an excellent job auto-optimizing campaigns. Checking to see whether everything is running smoothly is important as it will help you see what works and also add in any new insights you have gained during your existing or upcoming ad campaigns. Also, no matter how amazing your campaign is, you always need to monitor its performance. No unattended campaign lasts forever even in the most ideal of situations.

When reviewing campaigns or monitoring its progress, always ask yourself:

- Where can you see your Facebook campaign results?
- How else can you optimize your campaigns based on the current insights?

Facebook Ads Reporting in the Ads Manager

The Facebook Ad Manager is the easiest way to review your campaign performance. With the ad manager, you can filter your campaigns by dates, objectives, and zoom in on any campaign to see its performance based on its ad set.

You can also set the correct date range when looking for reports and compare different date ranges to see how your campaign has performed over time; you can select a date range of 7 days. Longer campaign periods could change your metrics making it a little difficult to understand and assess recent campaign performance.

As you look at the Campaigns tab in the Ads Manager, you will see the reporting table with different metrics such as:

- Cost-per-click.
- Cost-per-conversion.
- Impressions.
- Unique Link Clicks.

This is where you can get an overview of all your Facebook campaigns performance.

You can also select a specific campaign by clicking on the checkbox in front of the campaign name. Here, you can also navigate the Ad Sets and Ads tabs to view the performance of every individual campaign unit.

The awesome thing about this page is that Facebook automatically displays the most useful data for each campaign.

Managing Your Ad Report's Columns

While Facebook displays the most amazing ad metrics, generally you can still customize the ad reports according to your needs. You can do this by clicking the Columns menu to choose between different ad reports to change the metrics.

You can select pre-set reports or just create a new customer ad report by clicking on "Customize Columns."

Facebook Ads Manager allows you to see many different metrics. Here are the most important and insightful report metrics you can look into. The ad report metrics depends entirely on your goals and objectives; so of course, you can change it according to your needs.

- Performance: Results, Result Rate, Reach, Frequency, Impressions, Delivery, Social Reach, Social Impressions, People Taking Action, Positive & Negative Feedback, Amount Spent, etc.
- Engagement: Post Engagement, Post Comments, Post Shares, Page Engagement, Page Likes, Page Mentions, Event Responses, Check-Ins, Offer Claims, etc.
- Clicks: Link clicks, Unique Link Clicks, CTR, Social Clicks, etc.
- Messaging: New Messaging Conversations, Messaging Replies, Cost per New Messaging Conversation, etc.
- Media: Video Average Watch Time, Canvas View Time, 3-Second Video Views, 10-Second Video Views, 30-Second Video Views, Video Watches at 25%, Video Watches at 100%, etc.
- Website Conversions: Website Leads, Website Searches, Website Adds to Cart, Website Registrations Completed, Cost per Website Conversion, Cost per Website Purchase, Website Conversion Value, Website Custom Conversions, etc.

- Apps: Desktop App Installs, Mobile App Actions, Mobile App Adds to Cart, Mobile App Purchases, Cost per App Install, etc.
- On-Facebook: On-Facebook Purchases, Leads (Form), Cost per On-Facebook Purchase, etc.
- Offline: Offline Leads, Store Visits, Offline Purchases, Offline Ads to Cart, Cost per Offline Purchases, etc.

Once you have created the ad reports you need, don't forget to save them! You can also set any new report as the default option.
- Advanced reporting with Campaign Breakdown.
- Apart from the campaign metrics you can view on your Ad Manager reports, you can also take your reporting routine to a different level by using the Breakdown menu.
- With this feature, you can look at your metrics by using:
  - Delivery: age, gender, location, browsing platform, platform, device, time of day, etc.
  - Action: conversion device, destination, video view type, video sound, carousel card, etc.
  - Time: day, week, two weeks, month.

You can select different criteria from each of the sections above.

With the campaign breakdown, you can understand the goals of your campaign effectively and answer plenty of questions such as:

- The ad placements that works the best.
- The times of day or weekdays that deliver the most conversions at the lowest cost.
- The best-performing target countries.

To categorize your ad campaigns using the different criteria, you need to select one or more Facebook campaigns first. Next, select the criteria you want to focus on from the Breakdown option. Because Facebook Ads have plenty of reporting options, take your time to explore them. In time, you will gain a better understanding of the process and what ad metrics are important to look for your brand and optimization.

Save & Automate Campaign Reports

With Facebook campaign reports, you can also schedule daily or weekly reports to be delivered to your inbox, and all for free. When you are done crafting a report using Facebook Ads Manager, you can save the report and send to your inbox periodically.

All you need to do is click on "Report" located next to your account name.

Go to "Save new report..." and a small window prompt will appear where you can input the name of the report as well as set it up to be sent either daily, weekly, or monthly. Usually, a weekly report would suffice unless you want to track specific daily activities on your ad campaigns.

Chapter 8: Psychology of Facebook Ads

The psychology of Facebook Ads: what do people think when they look at your ad and what do people look for when they're on Facebook. Specifically, what is your audience looking for?

Content nowadays is driven visually. Consumers rarely buy anything without having a look at what they are purchasing. More often than not, people prefer trying it, touching it, holding, and smelling, and so on–basically using all their senses. With online retail, we cannot do much of touching and trying. It is usually a visual representation of a product.

Online images have come a long way. From the mediocre product photo or photos, e-commerce sites have evolved to enable a much deeper consumer experience to allow customers to understand the product they are purchasing–even without the need of touching or feeling it.

A good visual representation of a product will increase purchase rates, and that is why marketers need to work twice as hard to ensure their products come alive via excellent photography, display, graphics, and product description.

In a world where everything is becoming more and more visually driven (think Instagram and Pinterest), consumers can now take photos of a product and post it online. People take images of food, of the venue, of decorations, of buildings, and so on until we get a good idea of where the place is, and even the street it is on (Google StreetView) before even physically going there on their own.

Places like TripAdvisor allows both the management of a property as well as the patronizing customers to post pictures, and viewers can see what it is really like. Most people visiting the website often click on images taken by visitors instead of the management photos as it gives them an unpolished view of the place.

Instagram, being a visual app, has enabled people to build businesses just by posting images of their products and services on it. The more visually appealing an image, the more likes, the more reposts, and the more comments.

In this chapter, we will focus on images and what they can do to your online site, increasing your business, and increasing the conversion rate.

If you are selling a product or service, then you must have images of very high quality. In fact, any website in 2017 and beyond must have good quality design and pictures if they want to continue staying at the top of SEO rankings.

Too many websites attempt to sell their products with very low-quality images. This puts consumers off, and they wander to a competitor's website, who can offer a much better visual representation of their products.

1. Alternate & Detailed Views

You want to entice customers to purchase your product. Apart from a single photo, give users views from different angles as it can show character and carry a brand. A great example of thoughtful and visually appealing photography would be by Poplook, a clothing brand. The website gives you a default image of the product in full size and it also shows your clickable thumbnails of the product in different positions and angles. Check it out for yourself by going to Poplook.com

2. Context

Context matters when selling a product as it gives users an experience of using or wearing a product. You can show the product in its context. Following the example of Poplook, they also have a zoom in function and you can see the details of the clothing. There is also a short video of a model wearing the clothing item.

3. Avoid Unrelated Stock Photos

People pay attention to images. When websites were new, stock photos were regularly used to compliment content on a website. However, as websites keep evolving and users' tastes, interests, and levels of interest keep changing, people want to see more genuine content.

A website can create better authority in its field and increase traffic simply by using real people. Not models posing in stock photos but actual scenarios in their office space, road shows, venue, events, and so on. Purchasing stock photos will not do much nowadays. If you use stock photos of models in suits shaking hands or looking randomly into a computer, you are oblivious, and you think your customers are gullible. Genuine pictures showcasing the lifestyle of your company, your employees, the surrounding of your firm is one hundred times better than regular stock photos.

4. Focus Attention on Your Products

Did you know the eye focuses on a certain item when viewing an image? Tracking the eye movement of users when they view images on your website gives you an insight into human perception, which can be used in the design of your advertising, promotional, and marketing material.

This research conducted on eye tracking shows where men and women look and for how long, when viewing a product.

Even how products are placed in a supermarket can show how people look at items in a store or where their focus goes first.

These valuable insights can give you a good idea of how to design your online website and what images to place first in order to attract the user to buying your product or subscribing to your service.

5. Utilize Rotating Images

360-degree rotating images provides a user a whole new view of the product. This technology is a bit expensive, so it may be better suited to you if you are selling a high-end product such as cameras, laptops, vehicles, branded shoes, and so on, this 3D rotating feature will definitely boost your conversion rate. There are many design companies that offer this kind of specialization and there are also do-it-yourself built-in plugins and programs that enable you to do this on your own.

6. Product Images Located in Search Window Boost Conversions

Product images used in dropdown search results also give an extra boost for conversion rates. This increases the customer's likelihood of purchasing a product, because again you are using a visual aid to guide the customer in making a quicker decision of which product to purchase. It makes searching for products easier thus speeding up their time in making a decision. It also makes a customer feel like they have an increased sense of what they want based on what is available on your site.

Many companies have expressed their finding that using the product images in the site's dropdown search bar, we get a 100% lift in conversion rate among shoppers who use site search." Image-based search results have been shown to increase conversion rates and sales in online shopping and e-commerce sites.

7. Human photos on a Landing Page Increase Sales and Conversions

Adding a human face to landing pages increases conversion rates as well. People want to connect with a product or service and having a human face at the very beginning of their visit to your site makes them feel that they are part of the brand. This is especially true for brands banking on the human emotional quotient.

Again, pasting a random photo will not do. Always use real situations–something you know your users will do with your product or service. Think about why they would want to visit your site and give them that image in their minds. Flint McGlaughlin from Marketing Experiments says, "A strong face as the primary means of greeting visitors gets a strong reaction that polarizes conversion rates. Never put up a face photo that hasn't been thoroughly tested. It needs to be the right face."

Banking on this statement, think about who your users are, and even if you are using models in your photos make sure they represent your clients. No point putting in a Caucasian face when your target market is an Asian audience.

8. Step-by-Step Images

Step-by-step images work great for instructional blog posts. The PioneerWomanCooks started off as a blog and it's a good example of a blog which featured good quality step-by-step images of recipes. Viewers of her site related to her blog posts because the content was easy to read and fun and the images helped home cooks everywhere understand how their cooking should turn out just by looking at the pictures. Other blogs about recipes also feature images, but it is usually image upon image of the cooked recipe, just from different angles.

If you own and operate an instructional or DIY blog, harness the essence of step-by-step images. Your readers will thank you for it.

Depending on what your product or service is, having quality images is always the right way for marketing. Depending on your budget, you can increase the UX (user experience) by including images on the search results or adding in a 360-degree feature or even a video.

Nobody wants to read a post without images. It is too boring, especially now when readers want information fast. Without images, your posts will encounter less reading. You want more people to read your content and watch your videos. The more they read or watch your content, the more they will like you, and the easier it will be for you to bridge a connection with them. So, always use images in your blog posts.

Conclusion

All the information discussed in this book is really a beginner's guide to understanding the most important facets of an ad campaign on Facebook from creating a campaign, setting up the right creative elements, identifying and targeting your audience, as well as analyzing your campaign's performance.

Despite all this, you must know that advertising, especially the online version, is not a one-size-fits-all kind of marketing. You need to apply what you learn, observe, and test for each ad campaign to the next one so your effort and expenditure pays off. Every business is different. Only you will know the intricacies and nuances of your unique business and how to leverage them with your marketing strategy. Only you will know how your customers respond, and how to apply what you learn effectively.

Facebook Advertising is a must-have marketing tool, especially if you are conducting business online in any capacity. Who knows what other new platforms will exist 5 years from now? Whatever it is, as a marketer, you must take hold of all new and upcoming advertising avenues to reach greater and greater heights in your advertising strategy.

Book 2:

SEO for Growth

-In 2019-

Strategies to Stay Ahead in the Changing World
of Digital Marketing

By Matthew Bartnik

Overview

These days, effective SEO is more important than ever before!

- Search engines have never been smarter or more efficient
- New websites are being created every day, so there's never been more competition for search engine rankings
- User experience is the number one focus for all major search engines and platforms
- Old tricks to hack Google's search algorithms like keyword stuffing and excessive backlinking are no longer effective and may do more harm than good.

What does this mean for you?

To stay relevant and to edge past your competition, you have to change your understanding of SEO. This book will help you update and revamp your SEO strategy taking into account big changes and trends in the erratic world of digital marketing.

Here are some Key Realities that this Book Addresses:

Mobile first is here: we have crossed the threshold where more people are browsing and searching in mobile format than in desktop, and this trend will only continue. Google is, and has been focusing all their optimization efforts on the mobile experience. There are also more "mobile" devices than ever, and Google adopts a nuanced approach that varies from device to device. This book will teach you how to optimize your SEO strategy for Google's Mobile First Indexing Plan.

It's not enough to simply have a passable mobile version of your site. Google is giving preference to content and websites that are best optimized for the mobile experience and perform best in various mobile formats. While you shouldn't neglect the desktop format, and the implications will vary from industry to industry, Mobile First is here, and it's only going to continue in its trajectory.

Artificial Intelligence is here Including Alexa, and voice search. While AI as it relates to SEO is still in it's infancy when compared with its incredible potential, it is one of the most important trends to be adapted to. We will talk about practical strategies for how to optimize your site and your content for AI integration and especially Voice Search Platforms like Alexa and Siri which are at an unprecedented level of popularity and adoption.

Content matters more than ever—this means quality, not just quantity. It used to be that if you stuffed enough keywords into your content and had enough backlinks and played the SEO hack game, you'd be able to rise to the top quickly. However, Google has gotten a lot wiser and rendered a lot of those practices ineffectual. In fact, they are so focused on User experience, that if they detect abuse or spam-like behavior, they will punish you by pushing you further and further down their rankings or even blacklisting you altogether.

We discuss in great detail how to build a robust and effective content strategy that will be enduring and will always win in the long run. What matters most is that you have content that people like. This means its streamlined, topical, well-written, and well formatted/presented. Rather than plastering your website with hundreds of half-baked articles and listicles, focusing on quality will guarantee the optimal user experience which Google will quickly realize and boost your rankings accordingly.

Google's featured results have changed the game. Also referred to as "Google Snippet," this is the featured result that appears at the top of the search results and seeks to answer the user's question directly so the user doesn't have to actually click on any links. This is an ever-growing trend. It is estimated that as many as 30% of search results are answered by Google Snippet. This means, if you can optimize to become one of those featured results, you may gain considerable ground over your competition. This book discusses how to optimize for google snippet. You want to be able to answer questions where the user will want more information. You want them to click on your link, so you want to be featured, but you also want the user to want more information. This largely comes down to the question at hand. We discuss all this in detail in a later chapter.

- You will learn about all the tools you should have in your tool belt and the pros and cons of each including:
- Mobile Optimization, and Geolocation featuring
- PPC and Paid advertising
- Social Media Marketing
- Content Marketing and branding to Maximize Search Engine Optimization
- Influencer Marketing

This book gives you a thorough understanding of SEO and how it worked in the past and how it's changing for the future.

You will be able to develop a highly effective SEO strategy that accounts for the biggest changes and trends in the industry and be able to maximize your ROI for the money you invest in SEO and Digital marketing for your brand.

Introduction

Have you ever Googled yourself? It can be a scary experience for some, but an eye-opening event for others. For most people, when they Google themselves, they find hundreds of thousands of 'hits' online, whereby the search engine knows Facebook, Twitter, Instagram, and LinkedIn accounts, along with collages of photos of yourself and relatives that have found their way to the Internet. Even those with unique names may find tens of thousands of articles online mentioning either their first or last names in some order. While this may be an unnerving experience for some, others view it as an opportunity to showcase their products and services online, and as such, may profit greatly from the ranking Google chooses to place your product or service in their results page. This book is designed to give readers a background on how search engine optimization (SEO) works and will allow the reader to navigate Google's new algorithms for ranking search engine results. Not only is this a useful tool for marketing purposes, but it is also a way for entrepreneurs and small businesses to increase their online exposure.

This book is designed to give the reader an introduction into how search engine optimization works, along with a basic background on how it developed in this manner. Finally, this work is designed to show the reader how search engine optimization (SEO) will work in the future and how you can organize your content, business, and strategy along future SEO practices. The first chapter of this book will provide you with an introduction to SEO, along with the history of SEO.

It will also illustrate the nuances of how SEO operates so that the reader can possess a fundamental understanding of this technology for their business endeavors. This part of the book is important because it gives the reader a strong foundation on SEO's algorithmic complexities in a simplified manner. The second chapter of this book discusses rankings in SEO searches. Essentially, this chapter touches upon how Google puts your website higher up on the list of hits when somebody types in a phrase in their computer. Let's be frank: nobody searches through Google beyond the first hundred hits. Though there may be a million results if you type in a certain phrase, few people go beyond the first five pages of results in Google.

This book's third chapter deals with content marketing. It will show the reader how to make content effective when it comes to online marketing purposes. It will also touch upon the subject of influencer marketing, and provide examples of how it can be a useful tool for future entrepreneurs. Finally, as many of us already know, mobile devices are slowly replacing laptop and desktop computers as primary tools for Internet shopping, research, and browsing. Chapter 4 deals with advances to mobile SEO strategies, along with how you can use it to hit Google's first page when browsing on your mobile device. This chapter also touches upon the advances in SEO technology and how it will likely work in the future. At the end of this work, there will be a glossary, where the reader can easily look up any technical word or term found in this book. Those words with specific definitions will be in bold throughout the book. So, without further ado, let's take a look at how SEO works and operates every time a user searches something online.

Chapter 1: How Does SEO Work?

There are billions of searches on Google every single day, ranging from Facebook profiles to buying books like this one on Amazon. However, as hinted in the previous section, the vast majority of the searches conducted on Bing, Yahoo, and Google are never seen. Let's imagine that John wants to buy an iPad online. Naturally, he will search among known vendors of iPads, such as the Apple or Amazon websites if he wants a new one, or Craigslist and eBay if he is looking for a used iPad at a lower price. Alternatively, he may search on Google for 'iPad,' finding 1.2 billion hits online within half a second. Not bad, but if you are even 1% down on the list of advertisements selling iPads, then you are out of luck. According to some studies, the vast majority of content on the Internet never gets seen by anyone. Some studies illustrate how only 8% to 9% of all content is actively used. Everything else gets thrown away in a large pile of nonsense online along with everything else. So how do you ensure that your content fits into the 8-9% of 'haves' and not the 91-92% of 'have nots?'

The first thing you should know about SEO is, well, what it stands for—**search engine optimization**. SEO is, first and foremost, a process. It is the *process* by which search engines optimize your webpages and websites to get traffic on their sites, such as Bing or Google. Each search engine has its own algorithm determining the ranking of their sites. However, because this is a process, the site developer may be able to use it to their advantage. Below is a good way to think of how SEO works. Imagine that search engines, such as Google, are like filing systems in a library with billions of books and trillions of pages. Unlike the Dewey Decimal System that most libraries in the United States employ to catalogue their tomes, Google searches through each word in every book to determine the order of the webpages in their search engine. Suppose you want to learn more about Mount Vesuvius. If you were living in the 1950s, the most readily available information would be found in a library. So you'd walk to the library and on a calling card, write out the topic you were looking for. Topics could range from Pompeii to Geology, depending on what type of information you wanted regarding Mount Vesuvius.

SEO works slightly differently: instead of cataloguing books by topics in the way the Dewey Decimal system operates, SEO searches through every single page in each book in the library to determine which pages contain 'Mount Vesuvius' or closely related words in their writing. However, these results are not returned in a random order. Search engines use complex algorithms to determine what you are looking for in a reliable and predictable manner. In fact, most search engines are so good at this that the vast majority of people do not need to scroll beyond the first two pages of hits on Google for them to find what they are looking for. To be sure, each search engine's algorithm is proprietary, meaning that it is not open to the public, so nobody really knows exactly how they rank their web pages and search results.

However, even though their SEO algorithms may remain secrets, we can more or less figure out what search engines like Google use to rank their search results.

The order of Google's results when the user types in a word or phrase is called the **Google Ranking Factor**. The Google Ranking Factor (GRF) is a series of variables that Google uses to 'rank' each result every time a user searches for a word or phrase. The GRF accounts for multiple variables, some of which you may not be able to control, such as the age of the link. Other variables relate to whether the search result is in the title of the webpage, domain registration length, content length, and so on. So how do you increase your odds of having your webpage pop up in Google's first page of search results? The first thing that the user must do is to make it easy and readable for the search engine to know what your webpage is talking about so that your website can pop up on Google's top search results. Second, the user must make sure to show Google that their webpages are worthy of being ranked by Google when a user searches for their keyword.

Let's suppose that Jorge is an up and coming artist who paints vibrant, surreal portraits of downtown Chicago, and wants to display his portraits online so that he can sell them to customers. He wants to create a name for his budding business and decides that playing off of the Curious George kids' series, *Curious Jorge* is a decent name for his business. Now if searchers on the Internet look for *Curious Jorge*, they likely will not find his paintings because he has no Google footprint yet. So Jorge needs to put himself in the shoes of those looking for surreal paintings of Chicago. They may search for 'Vintage Paintings of Chicago for sale,' or 'Colorful Portraits Chicago,' and so on. Once he figures out the key words that users will be searching for online, he should visit **Google Analytics**, a website governed by Google that tracks and reports website traffic using the Google search engine. While there are many other analytical sites out there, Google Analytics is the most widely used tool on the Internet for such purposes. While eventually, Jorge would have to pay for the use of Google Analytics, he can initially begin for free and get to know his customers in a more nuanced and compartmentalized manner.

Google Analytics allows Jorge to determine who is searching for *Curious Jorge* online using the Google platform. It illustrates searches, clicks, and their percentages, but also *how* they use Google, be it on a mobile device or on a laptop. If Jorge sees that the vast majority of the people searching for *Curious Jorge* are doing so on a mobile device, then he would adjust his webpage accordingly. Google Analytics, creepily enough, can even narrow down the zip code and even neighborhood of the users searching for a specific keyword. Naturally, if Jorge is based out of Chicago and paints images of the Windy City, then he would like to focus his advertisements and the general 'look' of the webpage to clients based in his hometown. Furthermore, Google Analytics can show Jorge how long a user stays on a webpage. If they are spending two seconds on his website, he can be assured that they are not paying attention to what he is selling. But if Jorge sees that they are on the 'About' section of his website for a minute, then he knows that they are reading his biography.

Google Analytics also measures what is called the **bounce rate** of a webpage. The bounce rate is the percentage of users who visit a particular website and navigate away from the site after viewing only one page. Essentially, it's the number of people who view your webpage by mistake. Google Analytics also allows the user to "connect Google Analytics with Optimize, Surveys, Tag Manager, and Data Studio so you can quickly get the insights you need to deliver timely, relevant customer experiences" (Google Analytics 2018).[1] If Jorge's business takes off, then he would also use Google Analytics to conduct surveys and publish advertisements to further optimize the user's browsing experience. We will analyze these later on, but for now, it's good for the reader to know how useful Google Analytics may be for the budding entrepreneur, and how it builds a complete picture for Jorge of what users are searching for when it comes to his paintings.

Let's suppose that Jorge searches on Google Analytics for the typical search results, such as 'paintings of Chicago.' He will find monthly searches for the keyword or phrase, along with what's called the **parent topic** of the keyword or phrase. The parent topic is a way to determine if a search can be ranked for a topic keyword. So, for instance, let's imagine that there were only 50 searches for the exact phrase 'Vintage Paintings of Chicago for sale' in Illinois over the past month.

---

[1] Information taken from https://marketingplatform.google.com/about/small-business/.

Jorge's market in that sense is pretty small. So he checks out a parent topic of the phrase, finding that over twelve hundred people searched for 'Vintage Chicago Paintings.' Though this may be a more general topic, it is what people seem to be searching for, as it is more general than 'Vintage Paintings of Chicago for sale.'

By using similar parent topics, Jorge then knows what he must be including in his webpages to attract more customers. In this example, he sees that adding 'for sale' in any of his webpages simply isn't increasing traffic to his website. It is therefore in his best interest to simplify the language in his sites by simply titling his pages as 'Vintage Chicago' or 'Chicago in Twilight,' rather than describing any of his works or tagging 'for sale' at the end of the title pages. If Jorge is working on the 'About Us' section of *Curious Jorge*, then he would make sure to use the term 'Chicago Vintage Paintings' much more often than 'Vintage Paintings of Chicago for sale' because he knows the former gets 1,200 hits monthly while the latter only manages fifty searches per month.

In the past, this type of SEO that Jorge is incorporating was much more important than it is now. Over the past several years, search engines have become increasingly adept at determining what the searchers are looking for when they type in a keyword or phrase. This means that queries such as 'Vintage Paintings of Chicago' and 'Vintage Paintings Chicago' may ring in at a similar strength in Google's rankings, rendering this type of SEO a bit dated. The author can only assume that search engines will only get better in the future with this type of technology. It is also of specific interest to the reader that it is not worth it to try to cheat the system, because, after all, you are attempting to sell your product to humans and not robots.

For example, if Jorge figures out that 'Vintage Chicago' is a phrase that is quite popular, he should not simply title his artwork as 'Vintage Chicago Vintage Chicago Vintage Chicago Vintage Chicago Vintage Chicago' over and over again! This unnecessary repetition on keywords is known as **keyword stuffing**, and will not help you sell your product. While this may help your Google rankings, it will not translate into more sells, which, after all, is the whole point of Jorge's business. By the same token, he should not state in the 'About Me' section of his webpage that he is an 'Artist in Chicago making Vintage Chicago prints, and Vintage Chicago paintings, and Vintage Chicago photographs.' Again, while this unnecessary redundancy fools the computer, it will not convince buyers to purchase your product or service. Your bounce rate will be through the roof with these types of scrupulous strategies. Remember that SEO is an optimization strategy for people and not for computers, so make sure not to use popular keywords where they don't belong.

Jorge can furthermore search for keywords among the top-ranking positions for each similar Google search. This is a good way for him to figure out which keywords are most popular within his niche topic of vintage Chicago paintings. If Jorge is clever, he will create a list of keywords that the vast majority of people within the region use to search for vintage prints of their city. Once he has this list of keywords and phrases, he can now figure out which ones are most popular among users. For example, 'Vintage Chicago' may be more popular than 'Chicago at Night.' With this knowledge, Jorge then matches his title pages on his website to these popular keywords or phrases. This practice is called **on-page SEO**. As the name suggests, on-page SEO, also called on-site SEO, is the practice of optimizing each individual webpage based off of relevant traffic from search engines. On-page SEO technically refers to the content and HTML source codes that can be optimized in a page, such as the titles of Jorge's artwork. This is very different from **off-page SEO**, also called off-site SEO, which refers to the strategies taken *outside* of your website to increase the traffic (and subsequent rankings) of your website.

Let's take a look at how Jorge can increase both his on-page and off-page SEOs. First, as we briefly discussed, the best way to increase on-page SEO is to title the page with a popular search keyword. He may also include words, such as 'sale' or 'for a limited time only' in his webpages to potentially increase traffic to these sites. There are two aspects of titling webpages online, and it is worth it to understand the difference. The first component of titling a page is called the **title tag**. This refers to the part of the Google search result that is shown in blue when you have not clicked on it and turns purple after visiting the webpage. The phrase or sentences below the title tag are known as the **meta description**. The meta description usually appears in search results under the title tag and is oftentimes found in black under the actual website. Below is a figure to help you understand the difference between title tags and meta descriptions.

Figure 1: Title Tags and Meta Description (Source: ResearchGate 2018).[2]

In the figure above, we see that the user searched for the missing Malaysian Airlines flight from 2016. In this example, the first two hits were from ABC News and Sky News, both having similar titles to what the user searched for, which was 'Missing Plane MH370.' As the reader can see (and has probably noticed when surfing online), the title tag for ABC News is purple, meaning that the user has already clicked on that article. However, the title tag for Sky News is still blue, meaning that the user has not clicked on that link yet. The meta description for both links remains in black, under the green hyperlink to the actual website. Google even bolds the

---

[2] Photo taken from https://www.researchgate.net/figure/Html-Title-tag-and-Meta-Description-in-search-results_fig2_277619792.

parts of the meta description that were searched for, further increasing the chances of the correct keywords appearing with each search. The reader will notice how the words 'Missing Plane' appear in the Sky News meta description in bold, but not its title tag. Despite the fact that it's not in the title tag, enough people have searched on Google for the missing plane and found their answers in Sky News that they are still in the top search results for 'Missing Plane MH370.' Additionally, notice how the links most often clicked on go up top. This optimization tells Google that your webpage is likely closely related to what the users searched for, despite the fact, as the reader may have noticed, that it may be in a different language (Greek, in the example above).

Now let's return to Jorge's example. If he is interested in optimizing the results for one of his paintings, it is in Jorge's best interest to use the title tag as the name of the painting tailored for the most optimal search result that is related to his painting. In these types of cases, Jorge can dub himself *Curious Jorge* and title his pages 'Vintage Chicago' only if that is the most popular keyword or phrase. He should also not try to cheat the system by calling himself the 'best' artist in Chicago, as that is likely unproven, and should not be represented in the title tag unless he's received numerous awards. Secondly, the meta description can also contain some of the most popular keywords or phrases, but Jorge must remember that they should be related to the title tag and not unnecessarily repetitive, as this will adversely affect his sales. The meta description should also describe who he is and what he does, rather than the paintings themselves. If Jorge happens to be an award-winning painter, then by all means, go to town! However, if he is not such an acclaimed artist (yet), then Jorge can explain how he 'combines surreal creativity with popular pictures of downtown Chicago in twilight,' if that's what is most popular among Google searches. A final note on the meta description is in order: make sure *not* to repeat the same words, as multiple hits of similar keywords do not increase your optimization results. Similar to writing for the SATs or ACTs, a good rule is to attempt to use the most elaborate keywords that describe your product or service, rather than using the same adjectives, such as 'good' or 'best,' over and over again.

Another aspect about on-page SEO is the actual content itself. It does little to have a popular title tag and a decent meta description if the content is lacking. For *Curious Jorge*, one would think that he would post photographs, surreal paintings, vintage prints, and the like on his page. Jorge may title each of his works, and potentially include quotes, testimonials, and reviews from previous customers who are happy with his work. He may also continue talking about his business as part of on-page SEO strategy to generate more attractive content and lure potential clients into visiting his pages. While multiple strategies regarding title tags and meta descriptions are important for optimizing your work, the most important part of SEO is the content itself.

Alternatively, off-page SEO requires a bit more online creativity. Jorge would have to make deals with other, more popular sites than *Curious Jorge* and convince them to encode links to his page on their websites. For example, if the website

Visit Chicago would like to showcase some local art, they may be willing to help out Jorge and offer a link to his webpage. What Jorge is doing here is incorporating a specific off-page SEO strategy, creating a **backlink** for his products. A backlink essentially is the link that refers the customer to Jorge's page. Backlinks can come in various forms, ranging from manually putting a link on another's website to posting on Facebook or Twitter the link for Jorge's paintings. In modern parlance, backlinks offer a vote of confidence from one website to another. If *Visit Chicago* is confident in Jorge's work and business strategy, a backlink to *Curious Jorge* is a viable way to illustrate their support.

Off-page SEO strategies, like using backlinks from other websites, are similar to word of mouth recommendations for the Internet. Jorge has to keep in mind that not all backlinks are created equal. Backlinks from unconventional websites or spurious connections among backlinks ultimately increase your websites bounce rate. Because of this, Jorge must make sure that the backlinks he receives from other websites are of good quality. In the example above, the website *Visit Chicago* will attract a lot of tourists and art aficionados, rendering it a quality backlink. The same would hold true for Chambers of Commerce in the Chicago area, art and photography shops, online retailers, and possibly museums. Consistently ranked as one of the best types of backlinks are those from the media. If a Chicago-based newspaper or television station is doing a commentary or editorial on artists in Chicago, Jorge's SEO strategy would be bolstered by piquing their interest. Naturally, this takes time, talent, and hard work, but it can be done, as local artists are often highlighted in journals and magazines. On the other hand, poor quality backlinks may include something like Jorge's cousin, Tim, and his website on mechanical parts for vehicles, and the like. These types of backlinks are spurious in connection and do little to boost either webpage. Other poor-quality backlinks include forums where anyone can post a link or blogs that are largely unread and unrelated to the product or service you are selling. Furthermore, Google sees this as a potential way to cheat the system and may punish your webpage by ranking your website lower online.

So how does Jorge develop and keep quality links from other websites? Here's a pro tip: check which websites have links to your competitors. For example, if Jorge's competitors are websites linked to *Romantic Chicago* and *Chicago Noir*, he would search on Google Analytics for their backlinks to other websites. In Google Analytics, he can search for a domain name or a URL. From here, Jorge would be able to discern which websites have links to *Romantic Chicago* or *Chicago Noir*, and, perhaps more importantly, whether they link to these homepages or are linking up to one specific product. Naturally, some of their backlinks would be links to Facebook and Twitter pages, but there may also be links to local newspapers, art historians, professional photography clubs, art shops, and so on. This would be a good place for Jorge to begin seeking backlinks from other valuable sources. When seeking these sources, it is in Jorge's best interest to have backlinks to his homepage,[3] where the user can view all of his products, along with a short 'About Me' section. If his website looks clean and professional, he will likely capture the attention of his audience.

Jorge must remember that he needs to give a reason for other webpages to create backlinks to his site. This may be *quid pro quo* if each party has something to benefit. For example, if Jorge strikes a deal with one website to put a backlink to his homepage, he may promote them on Facebook and Twitter. This is especially true if the product you are selling is complementary to another product, in a process known as **cross-selling** (e.g., if you are selling jams and jellies, you can probably find a local peanut butter producer who is interested in teaming up with you; the same holds true if you are selling staplers and another vendor is selling tape). Monetary gain is usually a good incentive for websites to put backlinks from one site to another, but there are other benefits to using off-page SEO. If there is a blog about artwork in Chicago, Jorge may want to approach them with his paintings. Other curators and art schools may be interested in displaying his artwork on their websites, especially if Jorge has ties to

---

[3] The alternative scenario here is to place a backlink to a specific product he is selling. This would work if *Curious Jorge* was a website selling many different things. For example, if Jorge was managing the website for a hardware store and there were hammer manufacturers interested in placing backlinks to their products, Jorge could do so easily, knowing that hammer manufacturers likely do not also produce ceramic tiles, plaster, or paint brushes that can also be found in a hardware store. If a user is selling a similar product across the entire website (such as paintings of Chicago), then it remains in their best interest to place backlinks to their homepage and not to a specific product page

them. While these gains may be considered a type of prestige for the art school, they may be converted into sales for Jorge. On this note, since backlinks can be tracked by using Google Analytics, then both sites can determine whether or not the backlinks have been useful in generating sales. If Jorge continues along this trajectory and finds a way to monetize these backlinks, he can try to be the 'preferred vendor' of certain blogs, art stores, camera shops, and so on.

As we can see, what Jorge is doing is contacting businesses and individuals in lateral niches that are not in direct competition with his business. It would make little sense for Jorge to try to get backlinks from *Romantic Chicago* or *Chicago Noir*, as they are his direct competitors. The astute SEO operative would also abstain from seeking backlinks from future competitors. So, if Jorge is serious about his artwork and wants to paint landscapes of Washington, DC or Boston in the future, he should not approach future competitors in these niche markets.

When optimizing your website for Google, a good strategy to keep in mind is to use words that people will be searching for online. For example, though Jorge may want to introduce himself by saying 'Welcome to my Website' or 'Hola Amigos,' he must remember that users will not be searching for these keywords or phrases if they want vintage posters of the Windy City. Make sure to abstain from these types of practices if you wish to optimize your website to its fullest extent. Relevance to the user's searches is what is most important in SEO, not introductions or pleasantries. This step is very important to make sure that you are targeting the right audience for the most exposure in keywords or phrases. However, remember that your goal is to get Google to understand what your page is all about. Once you have that, then, as the saying goes, content is king.

All of this begs the question, how does Google rank your website? As previously mentioned, their ranking system is proprietary, but they enact certain measures to track how your website performs. Google employs a three-step strategy to ranking websites, and if you are interested in understanding SEO for your business, it is good practice to know what Google is doing when it searches through your webpages.

1) The first step that Google uses to search through your website is called **crawling**. Because there is no central registry of all webpages, Google must consistently be searching for new websites and webpages on the Internet. After all, new webpages are being created every day, so it makes little sense to catalogue them. The process of discovering new webpages is called crawling. According to Google's support website, some pages are already known to Google because it has crawled them before. However, other webpages are "discovered when Google follows a link from a known page to a new page. Still, other pages are discovered when a website owner submits a list of pages for Google to crawl. If you're using a managed web host, such as

Wix or Blogger, they might tell Google to crawl any updated or new pages that you make" (Google Support 2018).[4] This means that there are two strategies to improve Google's crawling of your website. First, if you are making changes to an existing webpage, you can submit a new URL to Google, so that it knows to crawl through your webpage once again. The second way to do this is to use off-page SEO to link to your new webpage. This off-page SEO may come from your own website. However, Google warns "that links in advertisements, links that you pay for in other sites, links in comments, or other links that don't follow the Google Webmaster Guidelines won't be followed" (Ibid.). Furthermore, the reader should know that Google does not accept any payment to crawl a site more frequently to make it rank higher than it normally would.

2) The second aspect of Google's ranking system is called **indexing**. Once Google discovers a page by crawling it, the search engine seeks to understand what the page is about; this is called indexing. Now remember, this is a machine that is doing this, not a human being. Because of this, videos and images are catalogued using one of Google's algorithms, but

---

[4] Quote taken from Google's support website, found at https://support.google.com/webmasters/answer/70897?hl=en

they will never be as good as using words. Google can analyze words extremely well, but understanding what a photo is conveying is (still) not something machines do well. A good practice is to describe your content—even if it is prints of Chicago in twilight, as in the example of *Curious Jorge*—using words, while simultaneously depicting the artwork with pictures. By crawling websites, Google has created something of a library of webpages, called the Google Index, which stores all this information in many supercomputers. It is in the reader's best interest to take advantage of this index to attract Google's attention and get their computers to crawl your website.

3) Once your webpage is crawled and indexed, the final process that Google uses to spit out search results is **ranking**. Also called 'serving,' ranking is Google's attempt to discover the highest quality answers per each query or search. Because Google already knows that mobile phones are used for many queries, it will automatically account for location changes. So, for example, if someone is looking for the phrase *Curious Jorge* in Hong Kong, they likely will not find Jorge's Vintage Chicago website. However, if someone in Illinois is searching using the same keywords, they are much more likely to see Jorge's website pop up on their first page. This localization of search queries is simply one variable used by Google in optimizing content online.

According to their website, Google uses over 200 variables to determine the ranking of websites online. However, this three-step process provides a good background on how Google searches for sites, and it's necessary to know in order for you to maximize the optimization of your website content.

Now let's go back to *Curious Jorge.* If Jorge were to expand his business and begin taking photos and painting surreal images of New York, San Francisco, or Boston, he would repeat the process for each city. He would have to make sure that each title tag and meta description matches the cities he is painting. For example, he would not bother with titling webpages as 'Vintage Chicago' if his new paintings are of New Orleans or Miami. Rather, he would not only title them appropriately, but the meta descriptions would also include 'Jazzy New Orleans' or 'Sunny Miami.' Furthermore, he would make sure that the URLs for each webpage have the names of the cities in them, and would ensure that his actual postage address (which is likely still in Chicago) is toward the bottom of the webpage where it will not interfere with his SEO efforts in marketing his paintings to a different audience. A good strategy for Jorge would be to study similar sites and different regions for ideas on how to optimize his content. If he sees similar sites struggling with SEO, then Jorge may be able to expose their suboptimal planning for his gain. Remember that Google is *forced* to rank websites. Somebody has to be on top, and those who happen to have the right keywords in some unknown order will be on the bottom. If Jorge can optimize his content correctly, he will then be miles ahead of the competition.

Now that the reader has a basic understanding of SEO strategies and how Google searches the Internet for your website, it is time to go through some tips and tricks on what to do and what *not* to do when it comes to SEO. Below are examples of both good and bad SEO strategies, so the reader can know what to emulate and what to avoid doing when seeking to optimize their content. In order to end this chapter on a good note, let's start off with the bad strategies first.

Bad SEO Strategies:

Duplication of Content: The first temptation for many would-be SEO optimizers is to duplicate content from successful sites. This strategy is akin to copying your neighbor's test answers in grade school. While the principal won't be putting you in detention for your behavior, Google will not be ranking your work highly in their search results. The reason for this is that the content already exists in cyberspace. Because of this Google finds no reason at all to index your page higher than any others already in existence. Jorge, for example, will not benefit at all from copying the content of another famous artist in Chicago (or any other city) and post it verbatim on his website, because Google already sees that content on a more popular page somewhere else on the Internet. In this sense, Google is technically worse than the middle school principal who caught you cheating; you don't get put in detention, but your business will suffer in the future.

<u>Too Many Ads Above the Information</u> Another temptation that many bloggers, news outlets, and social media sites have is to put a bunch of ads above the information they wish to convey. Because these sites only generate income off of ads, they are naturally encouraged to have advertisements.

However, too many ads, pop ups, and scrolling ads really diminishes the value of one's content and will increase the bounce rate of your work. Ads, in general, are to be avoided unless you are not selling a product or service. Jorge is selling artwork, so his webpage should not have ads at all. However, if he were to have a blog or a social media site, then he would have to rely on advertisements. He would have to make sure that the ads are off to the side (as in Facebook) or below the content (as in most news outlets. Advertisements on Google are analyzed by their **click-through rate**, also called their click rate. As the name suggests, the click-through rate is the percentage of users visiting a webpage who click on a hyperlink for a particular advertisement. If you have too many ads on your page, you will find that this click-through rate will drop in consequence. When this rate drops too low, Google will rank your page lower, and you will receive less money from advertisements online.

<u>Relying on Invisible Text</u> This is another unscrupulous strategy that many websites and webpages implemented in the past. For example, if the website's background were white, a clever strategy would be to type in the most popular keywords and phrases also in white, hence concealing the text.

Invisible text is the practice of concealing information by ensuring that the text and background are the same color. This is a bad practice because should a user accidentally highlight the text, they would know that the site is not trustworthy (and, in all likeliness, post about the site on their social media page). Google and other search engines are also getting much better at distinguishing between text meant to be part of the webpage and invisible text. Finally, invisible text is probably the best display of inadequate content. You would be much better off increasing the quality of your content than relying on invisible text to synthetically increase your Google rankings.

<u>Keyword Stuffing</u>: We previously discussed how this practice may lead to suboptimal results, but it is such a prevalent and banal practice that it is worth illustrating how useless this strategy is when it comes to SEO. Repeating the same popular keywords over and over increases your Google rankings at the expense of sales, clicks, and advertisement value. Humans are very quick to recognize patterns, especially simple ones, and they will quickly jump off your webpage if they see you doing this. Furthermore, Google and other search engines are getting much better at recognizing increasingly high repetitive rates in some pages, which may also adversely affect your

webpage's rankings online.

<u>Too Many Ingoing and Outgoing Links</u>: What once was a decent strategy, and still may be for many web developers, has been overused in recent history. **Ingoing links** refer to those links that are found in other websites that direct them to yours. Sometimes these can be bought, but Google's algorithm seems to figure out really quickly which links are spurious in their connection, meaning that you will lose your ranking among their webpages. While Google's algorithm for ranking pages is proprietary, their system must have some sort of code that recognizes synonyms and will determine if a link on one website is unrelated to the webpage it is taking the user to. These sorts of ingoing links will likely trick Google's algorithm for a short time but ultimately suffer worse consequences later on when Google finds out your strategy.

The opposite is also true: **outgoing links** are those hyperlinks meant to take the user to another webpage. Having too many of these on your webpage is also bad as it indicates to Google that you may be accepting payment for having those links on your webpage. However, if you have to use outgoing links, it is always a good idea to add a **nofollow tag**. This 'tag' tells search engines not to follow your outgoing link. Adding nofollow tags on outgoing links essentially tells Google that you do not fully trust the outgoing link, and illustrates that your own webpage may be a tad more trustworthy.

Good SEO Strategies

As we saw with the bad SEO strategies, the general rule applies: be ethical online! The vast majority of bad SEO strategies stem from a lack of ethics, combined with the relative anonymity found online. However, if you are interested in selling a product, being honest with SEO is likely the best practice. Now we will take a look at good SEO practices that may help you build a better and more effective website.

Content is King: This is a popular saying in the Internet world for a good reason. A good analogy is the 9th grade student that is seeking to attract everyone's attention in the classroom to himself by using crazy and loud antics. Instead of attempting to obtain his peer's respect, he is attracting their attention. While this may work for a while, ultimately, his fellow classmates will not respect him as a good student. However, if he decided to seek his classmates' respect rather than their attention (which is relatively short), then he will be successful. The same logic holds true online. The attention-seeking behavior that some website developers use to get Google's attention can only take them so far.

Users will be unhappy with your website if it looks like **clickbait**, which is content whose main purpose is to attract attention and encourage visitors to click on a link to a particular web page. These types of websites have a very high bounce rate, which, in turn, decreases your Google ranking. The way to avoid falling into this trap is to festoon your pages with vibrant and rich content geared to what you are selling, be it an idea, a product, or a service.

Optimize For Voice Search: Kleiner Perkins is a company that conducts online Internet trends reports, and in 2016, they discovered huge increases in search queries on Google, with many users searching for websites using their voices instead of typing in a keyword or phrase into the search bar. Whereas in the past, there the voice recognition technology implemented by Google and other search engines was correct only a fraction of the time, now Google is increasingly adept at determining what you are saying when you speak into your phone. What this means is that in the near future, the vast majority of users will be using their voices to search for keywords and phrases that previously had to be typed into the computer or smartphone. Make sure to optimize your website to make it searchable via voice.

Now, to be sure, Google does much of this already, but it is in your best interest to optimize your website for the way people *speak* and not necessarily the way they *type*. To continue using the *Curious Jorge* example, users may type in 'Vintage Chicago' into their computers searching for prints and photographs, but they may speak into their phones 'Pictures of Chicago.' If Jorge is smart with how he optimizes his content, he will ensure to account for voice searches in addition to standard SEO practices.

Use Relevant URLs: As the reader may know by now, a **URL** (officially called Uniform Resource Locator), is the technical term for a web address, commonly beginning with 'www.' In the past, we have seen URLs with special characters, strings of numbers, and case sensitive lettering. However, if you are looking to increase your presence online, it is in your best interest to use shorter and more relevant URLs. Another tip related to this point is to use popular keywords and phrases in your URLs, as they will then be accounted for when Google searches the Internet for those keywords. Make sure to use keywords that accurately describe the webpage to reduce your bounce rate.

Additionally, while your webpage may have a sentence as a meta description or a tagline, it is best to keep the URL to the first few words of the page, as Google has indicated in the past that they don't give much credit to words later on in the sentences. While you may not always be able to use short URLs, a good trick is to keep the pages you wish to be most popular with the shortest (and most popular) URLs, and generate longer URLs for less valuable pages in your website.

Optimize for Mobile Searching: Probably the most important improvement to SEO has been the introduction of smartphones. Because people are now not physically tied to one location, they may be searching for products on their smartphones much more often than in the past. Partially because of this, we are seeing a (perhaps unnecessary) proliferation of apps for absolutely everything under the Internet sun. Check out the chart below from Stat Counter depicting the rise of mobile searches over time.

Figure 2: Mobile v. Laptop Searches (Source: Forbes 2017)[5]

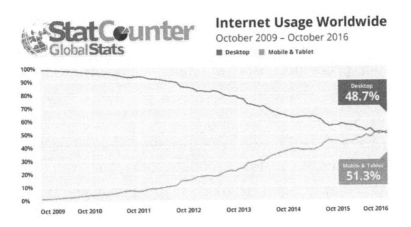

As the reader can see from the chart above, mobile searches have become increasingly common. While before 2009, mobile searches were extremely rare due to a combination of slow Internet speeds and a dearth of expensive smartphones, they have been gaining in popularity since their inception. Correspondingly, as mobile searches increased in popularity, desktop and laptop searches have decreased. Then, in 2016, what we all saw coming occurred –

---

[5] Chart taken from https://www.forbes.com/sites/johnrampton/2017/03/30/12-most-effective-seo-strategies-for-2017/#3491b54a6429.

mobile searches surpassed desktop searches for the first time in history. The smart entrepreneur eyeing this shift, must reorganize their SEO strategy to account for a more mobile SEO. To be sure, this does *not* mean creating another app! You can create an app if you think that users will benefit from it, but it does not replace the fact that your website must be appealing and photogenic when using Safari or Chrome on your tablet or smartphone.

Account for Geography: This tip only works if you are already in the mindset that most users will be searching for products online. The reader will recall that Google accounts for the zip code where searches are coming from, and with a more mobile audience, you can expect the same person to be conducting similar queries across multiple zip codes, cities, and even time zones. While they may not be taking their laptops with them, they surely will be traveling with their cell phones. The astute entrepreneur using SEO to improve their business would make sure to tailor their webpages for a more geographically interconnected audience. As online blogger, Gianluca Fiorelli, states, "Google is steadily moving to a mobile-only world. Mobile-first indexing seems like the inevitable consequence of a year (or more) almost exclusively dedicated to evangelizing and forcing a change of mindset from desktop to mobile" (Fiorelli 2017).[6] To continue the example of *Curious Jorge*, if he is attempting to sell his product in Chicago, it would be in

---

[6] Quote taken from Gianluca Fiorelli's blog found at https://moz.com/blog/seo-and-digital-trends-in-2017

Jorge's best interest to account for geographic shifts in his audience. Someone searching online for the term 'Curious Jorge' in New York City will likely not buy Jorge's artwork of his native Chicago. Because of this, Jorge must ensure that the most popular searches are stemming from neighborhoods and zip codes near his business.

The reader by now has a solid understanding of how SEO has developed over time, and what SEO strategies to implement for their website. The next chapter will discuss Google ranking in more detail, along with the impact artificial intelligence will have on SEO, and how you can use paid advertisements to your benefit. Chapter 2 will also illustrate how you can better develop your brand by using SEO correctly in your websites.

CHAPTER 2: OPTIMIZING YOUR RANKING

Have you ever seen the movie *I, Robot*? This Will Smith thriller is a science fiction film about how robots begin thinking for themselves and take over humanity. While far from unique, *I, Robot* touches on some topics of science fiction that have recently become more science than fiction. Rest assured that we are still a long way off from robots taking over our species, but we have trained computers to do some remarkable things. The next section of this chapter will discuss how SEO is developing and what you can do about it to remain ahead of the curve.

A key component of the movie *I, Robot* was the existence and prevalence of **artificial intelligence**, commonly known as AI. Science fiction movies, ranging from *2001: A Space Odyssey* to *The Matrix* oftentimes use AI as an antagonist to human desires (e.g., Hal in Kubrik's *A Space Odyssey*). However, when it comes to SEO, Google and other search engines are using a version of artificial intelligence to determine what exactly users are searching for when they type or say a keyword or phrase into their search engines.

This begs the question: how exactly does artificial intelligence work? While robots trying to kill us are a ways away, there have been significant advances in how they are programmed that allow them to 'learn.' Here's a very basic scenario of artificial intelligence: let's suppose that a student is writing an essay on Microsoft Word, and they accidentally type in 'teh' instead of 'the.' Many of us can automatically relate to this. Well, if you've used Microsoft Word lately, you'll notice that the incorrect word has been replaced with the correct spelling. The same rule applies to many other words. Now Google, Apple, and Android have taken this 'learned' word one step further. Let's suppose that Jack has a nickname for his sister, Jen, and instead of calling her Jen, he has dubbed her Chubbz to make fun of her. After typing in the word 'Chubbz' into his cell phone various times, he notices that his phone has essentially learned the word. In the future, when he texts his sister, his phone will automatically think he wants to spell 'Chubbz' even though he has only typed in a capital 'C.' The phone additionally will learn how to pronounce the word if he corrects it a few times when speaking into it. Pro tip: if you notice a dashed blue line under some words when you dictate to your phone, it's that the phone is attempting to discern what you are saying. If you want your cell phone to 'learn,' it is in your best interest to correct the spelling under this dashed blue line.[7]

The few examples above are rudimentary forms of artificial intelligence. Yet, AI is used for search queries

---

[7] Artificial intelligence differs from computing power in that AI can 'learn' and 'relearn' in a similar way to humans. Computing power is a computer's ability to perform extremely complicated calculations in a short period of time. This is how calculators work. More complex versions of computing power would include early versions of chess-playing computers that can compute thousands of 'if-else' commands in a second. *Deep Blue v. Garry Kasparov* is a commonly cited example of highly advanced computing power in chess games.

online in a similar fashion. This is how Google has taught its database how to learn in the past. Suppose that you want to teach Google what a traffic light looks like. There are certain characteristics of a traffic light: it has the colors red, yellow, and green; it is usually hung on a wire or placed on a pole, and there is a yellow or black casing around the traffic light; sometimes two lights are on at once, and so on. Google programmers 'teach' Google what a traffic light looks like by showing it millions of images of traffic lights from different angles and ranges.

If Google makes any errors, the programmers correct what it's misreading and continue on trying to teach it more and more things. This 'teaching' creates layers in Google that enable it to discern the difference between a traffic light and a stop sign. It is also with this teaching that Google can determine what someone looks like. Facial recognition technology has blossomed in recent years thanks to AI being used to recognize people's faces.[8] After teaching Google how to distinguish between objects, programmers sought to make it 'dream' an object. Some of the more hallucinogenic results are found below.

Figure 3: Google's Dreams (Sources: Gershgorn 2015; Tyka 2015)[9]

---

[8] Other social media sites, such as Facebook, use similar technology to ensure that no violent images or pornographic material are uploaded to their websites.

[9] Information taken from https://www.popsci.com/these-are-what-google-artificial-intelligences-dreams-look#page-2

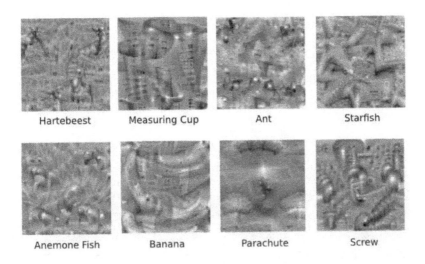

| Hartebeest | Measuring Cup | Ant | Starfish |

| Anemone Fish | Banana | Parachute | Screw |

As we can see, while humans may be able to distinguish bananas, parachutes, screws, and starfish quite easily, the result is a bit messier when teaching a machine. While we may be able to see starfish and ants in the images above, no human would say that this is reality. The computer cannot come up with a Platonic prototype of an image, despite 'seeing' them millions of times over. For example, comically enough, "when asked to create a dumbbell, the computer depicted long, stringy arm-things stretching from the dumbbell shapes. Arms were often found in pictures of dumbbells, so the computer thought that sometimes dumbbells had arms" (Gershgorn 2015). In order to combat this disembodied arms syndrome, programmers are trying to get Google to pull out patterns from what would be white noise, to create a process called **artificial neuron network**

(ANN). This ANN creates artificial layers that work on different degrees of abstraction, whereby the machine would pick up different degrees of contrast and patterns in shapes. Below is another image of Google's 'dreams' where programmers taught it to create a pagoda, only finding that since pagodas are based off trees, Google couldn't really tell the difference.

Figure 4: Pagoda v. Tree (Source: Gershgorn 2015

These 'dreams' are completely a neural representation of the computer's mind, based off seeing hundreds of thousands of pagodas (and trees). As we can see from the image above, the computer can create a central pagoda, with accurate coloring to a great extent, as they're usually red. However, it also mistakes and combines clouds and trees for other, smaller pagodas in the background, sometimes not being able to distinguish between trees and pagodas at all. As we can see, Google programmers are creating layer after layer of data in order to teach Google how to recognize images. Each of these layers are ultimately components of AI's whole, and "have to be crafted by people, and it takes time. Google had the bright idea of getting the pre-existing AI to create its own layers of code, and as it turns out, it's doing it a lot faster and more effectively than its human technicians ever could" (Andrews 2017).[10] In a sense, Google has become its own creator. And if search engines are creating minds of their own, then how in the world are you to optimize your content?

Self-teaching algorithms are very interesting, but how does it help you use SEO to further increase your rank in Google? As the reader may have guessed by now, this makes SEO more difficult to master, as Google itself is not a stagnant entity, but recreating and learning over time. The first step every SEO operative must keep in mind is that content is *still* king. Take a good look at the pictures above on what Google thinks are trees, pagodas, bananas, and parachutes. You can definitely see what Google was thinking, though it looks like a hallucinogenic dream. Let's take a look at an example: suppose that Sophia is looking to sell soy-based candles online and is calling her business *Soyphia's Candles*. In order to ensure that she is gaining traction online, she should employ all of the SEO strategies that we discussed in Chapter 1. However, since

---

[10] Quote taken from https://www.iflscience.com/technology/google-ai-creating-own-ai/.

Google is getting increasingly good at recognizing images (and even creating some of its own), Sophia ought to put some images up of her candles.

Here's the trick – Sophia may be able to make some truly spectacular soy-based candles shaped like boats, pyramids, and so on. However, and this is very important, Google will not recognize the pictures as candles (yet). Therefore, Sophia must put photos of her regular-shaped candles on her homepage, with the appropriate title tags and meta descriptions. She can, of course, sell candles shaped like Santa and Donkey Kong if she likes, but they probably shouldn't be the first candles Google, and the users observe when they click on *Soyphia's Candles*. Naturally, if she wants to sell these on her website, she is more than able to do so. If she uses her SEO correctly, then she would title the pages 'Santa Soy Candle' or 'Boat Soy Candle' and use these keywords in her meta description. This would ensure that those users specifically searching for a Santa looking soy candle find her page. If she sells candles that are cylindrical in shape, as most candles are, then she can put *photos* of these candles on her homepage, as Google is more likely to recognize them as candles and not as other objects (note the confusion with pagodas and trees above).

We must remember that the original purpose of AI in SEO is to create a better user experience and to tailor ads and websites to what the users were originally searching for. So far, this sounds like a congruent plan with what Jorge's artwork and Sophia's candles goals are: they want people looking for artwork and candles to buy their products. As marketers, their goals are congruent with Google's goals, but in order to optimize their webpages and content, they must make their processes symmetrical with Google's goals as well. The trick to doing this is to identify your niche market as narrowly as possible. That way you will be able to create content that is specific to the market you wish to penetrate. Using this logic, Jorge would attract those users seeking to buy vintage and surreal looking artwork of Chicago. That's pretty specific! Using these SEO strategies, his website can pop up first in Google's webpages. The same would hold true for Sophia: if a user is interested in buying soy candles online, she should combine elements of Chapter 1's SEO strategies with photos of her candles on her homepage. The reader must remember that Google is designed to create the best user experience for those who use it as a search engine. This means that if Jorge and Sophia's webpages have all the correct SEO, but do not provide a good user experience (e.g., Sophia is selling lamps and not candles), then Google will punish her by ranking her website lower in its rankings.

Now that the reader has a general idea of what AI is, here are some basic, and actionable, suggestions that can be used to improve your website, emails, and content. Let's begin with the basic tools that implement AI to improve your content (and writing) on your websites. The first tool is a bit basic, but worth using if you are typing anything in emails, websites, and blogs.

Grammarly: This is probably the most popular AI tool out in the market. Grammarly makes sure that everything you write, be it an email or a webpage, has no spelling mistakes. While Microsoft Word and other databases indicate which words are spelled incorrectly, it does not distinguish between grammatical mistakes nearly as accurately as Grammarly. Let's suppose that Sophia wants to post in Facebook a picture of her candles and a link to her website. Grammarly would immediately flag incorrect grammar, such as in the previous sentence where the author should have written 'on' instead of 'in' (and Microsoft Word didn't catch it). Grammarly also notes repetition in rhetoric, such as saying 'thank you' twice in one webpage or email.[11] This sort of **machine learning**, also known as natural language processing, learns from previously typed words and phrases, and, unlike Microsoft Word, can change organically.

Clearscope: Clearscope is quite possibly the most concentrated display of AI on the Internet. First, the bad news: you have to pay for it. And it's quite pricey at $300 a month. Now that we got the bad news out of the way, here's what Clearscope does for your business. It analyzes "the top 30 results on Google for any keyword you enter and then gives you data and actionable advice on how to write content that can compete with them. Part of the way it does this is by analyzing other common keywords that appear in those articles so that you can work them into your piece naturally"

---

[11] In a similar vein, email services, such as Gmail, note when the user writes the word 'attached' but does not attach a document, and sends them a reminder after they click 'send' just in case they forgot to attach something.

(Siu 2018).[12] Clearscope's algorithm measures the intent of the Google user rather than an exact match with the keywords or phrases. In essence, 'Vintage Chicago' may poll better among Google searches than 'Chicago art for sale,' but with Clearscope, *Curious Jorge* can worry less about keyword match, and more about the intent of the keywords. Siu elaborates, stating that this "means keyword stuffing [as defined in Chapter 1] is less effective and quality, well-written content is more likely to rise to the surface. In fact, you can even rank for keywords that aren't found in your article if you satisfy the intent of that query" (Ibid.). In order to drive organic traffic, Sophia and Jorge need content that is not only readable and clickable, but also relevant to what users are searching for – Clearscope helps users do just that. Through a combination of real-time search data and natural language processing (similar to what Grammarly uses), Clearscope helps create that organic traffic necessary for Jorge's and Sophia's sales to increase.

HubSpot: Here is another interesting tool for the entrepreneur. HubSpot automatically connects the entrepreneur's Facebook, Twitter, LinkedIn, and other social media sites together and analyzes the effects of a social media campaign on sales. For example, if Sophia's social media page displays a peppermint scented candle for the holiday season, she would like to know the effects of her Facebook campaigns on her profits. HubSpot allows her to track clicks from

---

[12] Information taken from https://www.impactbnd.com/blog/seo-ai-content-marketing.

backlinks on her Facebook and Twitter pages to her website, and those clicks to the 'buy' option online. In this sense, HubSpot implements what is called **multi-touch attribution**. Instead of simply counting the number of clicks a user makes taking them from Facebook, to *Soyphia's Candles*, to the page with the peppermint smelling candle, to the 'buy' option, to the credit card information, and to the 'confirm payment' option, this website tracks users' multiple clicks from one website to another, thereby tracking whether or not a Facebook post led to a sale. Similarly, HubSpot offers **cohort-based attribution**. This means the level of AI allows the user to track returns on advertisement spending over time. Through these means, Jorge and Sophia can effectively determine if their online advertisements are working. They can even micro-target their audiences at more specific levels to determine which zip codes are most profitable and what times of the day people are more likely to be buying artwork or candles.

There are many other apps designed to improve your SEO, ranging from Demand Jump (which analyzes customer behavior by developing algorithmic attribution models to determine what drives customers to 'buy or not buy' a product) to CoSchedule (which allows back-end ease when it comes to scheduling meetings). Both of these systems use AI to improve their algorithm, meaning that, similar to Google, their database learns from itself. Oftentimes this is called a 'smart' algorithm. Make sure to not confuse 'smart' algorithms with algorithms teaching other algorithms, *a la*

Google. The latter is a clearer example of AI than smart algorithms.

Paid Ads Vs. SEO

Now that the reader has a solid background on how AI works (and will operate in the future), let's take a look at some marketing strategies that Jorge and Sophia can take to increase their exposure online. Let's remember that marketing strategies are not SEO, but rather are essentially high-powered backlinks to *Curious Jorge* or *Soyphia Candles*. Below is an analysis of the pros and cons of paid advertisement versus SEO.

Paid Advertisement: Paid advertisement is a viable form of communication between Jorge and Sophia and their potential customers. Unlike SEO, which ranks pages in some sort of proprietary (and ever-changing) order, different rules govern paid advertisement. **Pay-Per-Click (PPC)**, also known as cost per click, is a way to measure the success of advertising online whereby the advertiser, such as Jorge or Sophia, pay the publisher every time a user clicks on their link.

Keep in mind that PPC is very different from a regular advertisement, such as in a newspaper. If you want to advertise in the *New York Times*, you would pay the editor a certain fee for publishing your advertisement and hope that people in their distribution lists see your company logo. With PPC, the process is different. The way it works is the following: every time a user clicks on your advertisement, a visitor is directly taken to your website. When this happens, you pay Google, or another search engine, a small fee, hence the name pay-per-click. If you manage to put these advertisements in the right places and your website operates smoothly, you should see a **return on investment (ROI)**[13] for the advertisement.

Pay-per-click has some seriously good benefits that should be analyzed as a viable option for increasing the online exposure of your brand. Here are the benefits of using PPC. First, it is good for those users who would buy something by clicking online (searchers). For example, if a user searches for 'soy candles' on Google, they may come up with millions of hits, but the top hits are almost always advertisements. Google knows this and marks them correspondingly, such as in the figure below.

Figure 5: Google Search for Soy Candles

---

[13] The return on investment (ROI) is the amount of money generated from a specific investment minus the costs of placing an action. This means that if Sophia spends $6 in advertising online but sells a candle for $14, then her ROI was $8.

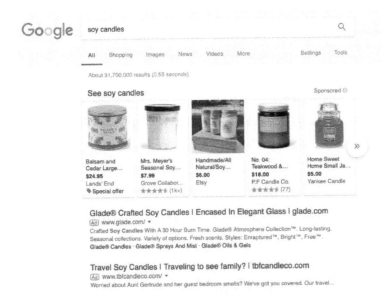

The author simply typed in 'soy candles' in Google, and received 31 million hits. However, only five images show up in the news feed. Let's notice a few things before we continue. First, look at how every image that we see in the screenshot *looks like* a candle. If the author had typed in 'skeleton shaped soy candles' we likely would not be seeing these typical cylindrical candles pictured in the image above. The second part of the image above that we should notice is how all five photos and the first two websites are advertisements, with Google marking them as such. This is called an 'organic' search. The user searches for soy candles and correspondingly receives a bunch of ads for that item. If the user had searched for 'Lebron James' or 'Derek Jeter,' very few, if any, ads would show up.

Because of this, PPC is *much more* effective than generic advertising on Google. This means that users tend not to mind having advertisements place products for them online, as long as they meet the requirements that they are looking for. If you search on Google what the weather is going to be like in Memphis next week, you likely do not want to see images of iPhones for sale on your search results. However, if Google sees that there will be pouring rain in Memphis, you may see ads for umbrellas and raincoats (and possibly a Marc Cohn song).

PPC especially benefits Jorge and Sophia as advertisers looking to sell their product online. They do not have to bother placing ads in Google where people are not searching for artwork or candles. They can tailor their specific brand to those who are searching for their products or something similar to what they are selling. This means that the pay-per-click rate works in their favor. Only those who are looking to buy artwork and candles are going to bother searching for these items in Google. Furthermore, as we previously saw, Google is getting increasingly good at determining the searcher's *intent* rather than the actual words they type in, meaning that if somebody searches for 'candles with wicks' online, multiple different types of candles will pop up. So every time a user clicks on one of *Soyphia's Candles* ads, she would pay Google a small fee. The reader may be wondering by now what is the typical fee for a click on one's advertisement online must be. While this generally changes depending on the industry (e.g., clicking on an ad for a car will be more than clicking on an ad for boots), they average at around two dollars a click. Housing and construction advertisements tend to be on the more expensive end, while dating apps and the like tend to be cheaper. In the author's (humble) opinion, PPC is only going to improve with time, because it benefits the small business owner, such as Jorge or Sophia, while *simultaneously* benefiting Google, as they can receive payment from thousands of vendors a second. Google can then reinvest that money back into their algorithms to perform even more tailored and unique searches for every buyer that shops online.

As the reader can probably imagine by now, Google does not rank advertisements at random. Google has its own PPC ranking system called Google Ads, formerly known as Google AdWorks. Every time a user searches for an item online, Google "digs into the pool of bidding advertisers and chooses a set of winners to appear in the ad space on its search results page. The 'winners' are chosen based on a combination of factors, including the quality and relevance of their keywords and ad text, as well as the size of their keyword bids" (Word Stream 2018).[14] Google uses two basic metrics to measure whose advertisement gets put first in line, called an **Ad Rank**. While we know what the metrics are, we do *not* know the algorithm used to quantify those metrics.

The first metric used to determine an advertisement's Ad Rank is the **CPC Bid**. This metric stands for cost-per-click bid, and measures the price advertisers pay when a user clicks on their ad. So, if Jorge's ad attracts twenty clicks, Jorge would have to pay for each click. The more he is willing to pay per click, the higher his CPC bid will be. The CPC bid is divided

---

[14] Information taken from https://www.wordstream.com/pay-per-click.

by the **Quality Score**, which is a rating of the 'quality' of the keywords and PPC ads. The 'quality' part of the equation is accounted by measuring the click-through rate, the relevance of the keyword to the ad, the actual landing page of the advertisement, among other factors, such as relevance of the URL and the history of the page. Assuming *ceteris paribus* (everything else being equal), the stronger your quality score, the higher your ad rank will be in Google.

PPC v. SEO

By now, readers will have a good grasp of SEO and PPC, but they may be stuck between a rock and a hard place. If they have infinite time and money, they can choose to increase both their PPC and SEO. However, most small businesses—or large ones for that matter—cannot afford to cover the costs of time, money, and resources on both SEO and PPC. So how do you know which option is the best for your business? This section seeks to answer just that question.

First, let's understand the differences between ads and organic SEO results. When Google spits out a search result, we must remember that paid ads appear above organic search results. The former is PPC, which has to be paid for by the advertiser, such as Jorge or Sophia. The latter, on the other hand, is free but requires a lot of time to get right—SEO. Implementing SEO strategies to boost your organic ranking in Google does not cost a penny, but will definitely take time away from your business or enterprise. Both Jorge and Sophia need to do some back-end calculations to determine which strategy works best for them. For example, if Jorge finds that artwork for advertisements never really sells well, he may opt for a strong SEO strategy. On the other hand, if Sophia sees that she can obtain a strong CPC ratio in her PPC, then she may choose to go the advertisement route.

Besides the relatively inexpensive costs associated with SEO, there are a few other benefits. A strong SEO strategy creates an awareness within Google of your company or business. This is a double-edged sword, however. One bad review can remain at the top of your Google rankings for a long time. Conversely, a string of good reviews can bolster user confidence in your product. This confidence builds upon credibility and trust. A small business, such as the one Sophia is running, has to rely on multiple and repeat customers, meaning that the better their reviews are, the more profits Sophia is likely to generate. In this vein, if Sophia sees that her small business is climbing up the Google ranks, she is already miles ahead of many other sellers in the same industry. That said, to *be* miles ahead of your competition requires a lot of hard work.

So, what if you don't have to compete with many others in your industry? Certain industries are hyper-geographically focused. Take wedding photographers for example. Very few wedding photographers are interested in traveling cross-country to cover a wedding. This means that if you are a wedding photographer living in the suburbs of Tulsa, you likely do not have too much competition. Thus, when somebody in Tulsa searches for 'wedding photographers near me' or 'wedding photography in Tulsa,' your page is much more likely to reach the top of Google's rankings. If this is the case, then the wedding photographer should employ a targeted SEO strategy, rather than struggling and paying for PPC.

Another interesting advantage to using SEO is an improved click-through rate. According to Marcus Miller, a "higher percentage of users click on the organic results. While there are exceptions to this rule, you will generate more clicks from a highly placed organic listing than from a highly placed paid ad" (Miller 2017).[15] This means that users implementing Google as a search engine tend to trust organic results much more than paid advertisements at the top of the page. Connected to this SEO advantage is another one worth a second look. There is a noticeable *sustainability* advantage with using SEO over paid advertisements. If you take your advertisement off Google, the ad goes away. However, with SEO, your website is ranked higher in search results because of the work you *previously* did, and is not related to how much you paid per click on your ad. This means that for your business, you should think long and hard about your business strategy. Suppose Sophia is only looking to sell soy candles as a part-time side gig. Should she bother with SEO or go straight to PPC? This author suggests PPC that way she can devote the rest of her time to doing anything else. On the other hand, if Jorge wants to make a living off of selling vintage prints, he

---

[15] Quotation taken from https://searchengineland.com/seo-vs-ppc-pros-cons-integrated-approach-274643.

should employ a strong SEO strategy.

We discussed a few of the advantages of using SEO over PPC, but what are the benefits of PPC? First, if you are looking to employ an SEO strategy, you must take into account that you'll be competing with giants, such as Amazon and eBay. If you see that your website is consistently ranked lower than these giants, you may need to rethink your strategy (perhaps selling *Soyphia's Candles* on Etsy may do the trick). Some businesses offer a completely unique product, such as Jorge's vintage prints of Chicago. These cannot be found anywhere else other than at *Curious Jorge*. Because of this, he does not have to compete with Amazon, eBay, or Craigslist. On the other hand, there are multiple vendors of soy-based candles, meaning that Sophia's competition in her niche is much stronger. Again, choosing SEO or PPC depends on your business model.

PPC offers a very targeted audience. Because of this, you are not competing against Amazon or eBay, as they sell everything, but rather against another, very niche market. This extremely targeted audience may be smaller, but much more receptive to paid advertisements in their results, as they searched for just that! Another advantage to PPC is time. Whereas developing website credibility and increasing your Google rank takes a lot of time, developing a paid advertisement may take a day. Using PPC in this manner may be a good way to rapidly increase your exposure online, especially if you are looking to sell products during the holiday season or Valentine's Day. Again, this depends much on your business model. Related to the speed of getting your products online, PPC is a good strategy if an entrepreneur is testing a product to determine how successful it may be. Because you get results relatively quickly, there are multiple ways to test your product to gauge its popularity quickly.

Here's another neat thing about PPC. Unlike SEO strategies that pit one website against another, PPC actually has a visual representation of the product you are selling (such as in *Figure 5*). If you are selling a visually appealing product, PPC may be precisely the strategy for you, especially if it is a unique product. If you are a lumberyard looking to sell 2x4s, a PPC strategy is likely not for you because 2x4s are not visually appealing. However, if your small business designs hand-made penchants, now PPC is a more viable strategy, as these can appear as visually-appealing advertisements on Google. PPC is additionally a good strategy if you are a small business selling many different items. While all candles may look more or less the same, if you are a jeweler with many different types of necklaces, earrings, bracelets, and rings, then you are consistently pumping out new products and product lines. This would render PPC a stronger strategy than SEO because otherwise, users would have to search for very specific keywords to reach your landing page.

The final advantage to using PPC over SEO is related to the advances in SEO that this book discussed in Chapter 1. Using PPC protects and hedges against changes in SEO algorithms employed by Google. Precisely because SEO algorithms change, websites "that have been optimized in one way can lose rankings -- and profits -- practically overnight. But when you pay for traffic, you're assured a steady stream of visitors, no matter what changes Google and the other search engines make" (Kumar 2012).[16] This reality is especially true if there are a lot of photos and videos on your landing page that may confuse Google's current algorithm. All of this begs the question: can you use PPC *and* SEO at the same time?

As the reader may remember from above, using both PPC and SEO is both costly (PPC) and time-consuming (SEO). If the entrepreneur has changed strategies or is looking to get a product off the ground quickly, then an oscillation between PPC for the new product, combined with SEO, later on, could be a good idea. Once users begin searching for the product online more frequently, the entrepreneur can remove the paid ads. Then, when there is another product that they wish to sell, they can repeat the process *ad infinitum*. Here's the trick with this strategy: the entrepreneur must switch strategies over and over again. This works if a business is selling different products all the time, or growing at such as fast rate that a new product line is in order every few months.

Some readers may be tempted to use both SEO and PPC at the same time. This is definitely possible, but, unless you have a very specific reason, it is generally not considered an optimal strategy. Not only does this tactic cost both time and money, your efforts may ultimately cancel each other out. Imagine if a user searches for soy candles online and sees both

---

[16] Quote taken from https://www.entrepreneur.com/article/223567.

a website found organically through SEO strategies *and* an ad for the same product placed there through PPC. It is in Sophia's best interest to have the user click on her website and save the cost of clicking through the advertisement, but that's not a guarantee. Ultimately, having your webpage pop up twice for one search cuts the effectiveness of both strategies by half, rendering this combination a suboptimal solution to online marketing problems.

By now, the reader should be familiar with the differences between PPC and SEO, along with having a general idea on what strategy they would be using for their business. There is a second part of SEO that we have purposefully been putting off—branding. This next section discusses how branding can develop your SEO strategy over time.

Branding and SEO

There are multiple ways to build your brand online. This section is going to discuss how you can incorporate this brand building into your SEO strategy. In order to understand branding online, the reader must have a foundational comprehension of **SERPs**. Search engine results pages (SERP) are essentially the landing pages for Google when a user searches for a query. In the vast majority of SERPs, the big names like Amazon, Etsy, and eBay dominate the Google field. The reader will do well to consider this first landing page on Google as prime real estate for SEO. While SERPs are a good topic to understand throughout the book, it is especially important for branding, hence the late definition for the term. The prime real estate of Google's first page leaves little room for many vendors that do not operate through Amazon, Etsy, and eBay.

This is where branding comes into play. As we saw from the AI section of this book, Google is consistently tinkering with its algorithm, attempting to determine what the searcher's intent is when they type something into the search engine. Google is using **featured snippets** much more often in its algorithm than it used to in the past. Featured snippets are select search results that are found at the top of Google's results. Instead of spitting out the top ten links like Google used to do in the past, now Google is attempting to guess what the user is asking when they type something into their search engine. This featured snippet tends to draw much more organic traffic than Google's old model of the most commonly cited websites. Below is a screenshot the author took when searching for 'why ice floats' on Google.

Figure 6: Why Does Ice Float in Google

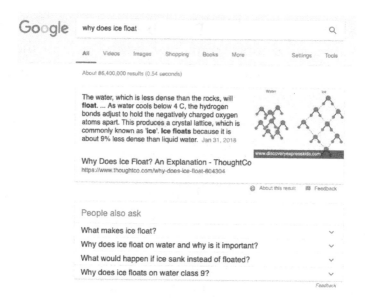

In the past, if someone had searched for these results in Google, the search engine would have simply spit out results. Now, Google is attempting to answer the question for you, using the most relevant and organic search results. This is both blessing and curse for SEO. If you happen to be www.thoughtco.com, then you're probably doing the wave, as your website came up first in this Google search. However, as seen above, there are over 86 million hits for this question, meaning that if your website is not in the top ten, you're likely not to get too many clicks through this search result. Here's the problem for SEO, users are getting their answers directly from Google, and not from other websites. In the example above, the user does not need to click on *ThoughtCo* in order to get an answer; they; they can figure out why ice floats just through Google. Google has speculated that it is currently a 60% to 40% split of those who click to those who do not. In the future, we can only guess that this will be closer to 50/50, as Google's predictive nature gets better. So how does this affect the entrepreneur?

The first thing to keep in mind is the type of industry the entrepreneur interested in SEO is in. If they are an 'information' website, whereby the searchers are seeking information, such as why ice floats, then they have competition with *ThoughtCo* along with a variety of other companies. On the other hand, if we are thinking of *Curious Jorge* or *Soyphia's Candles*, then they are not likely to suffer as much from Google's featured snippets. So, what is the best way to combat this 'less than organic' search results from Google? Branding, plain and simple.

The first thing that you should do when attempting to brand your websites online is to specialize. Specialization is the key to driving some sort of organic traffic. *Curious Jorge*, as a website dedicated to vintage prints of Chicago, is already pretty specialized, meaning that if someone searches for 'Curious Jorge' on Google, his website should pop up. However, if they search for 'Vintage Chicago,' which is likely a more popular search, then he would have to compete with other artists and print shops. After Jorge and Sophia specialize in their content and messaging, they must take charge of their message. For Jorge, this must mean why he is painting images of Chicago, and for Sophia, why does she like soy candles? The reasons are already there, but they need to go an excellent job in determining how they can relay that message to their customers. Remember, Google keeps track of how long users stay on a certain page, meaning that Jorge and Sophia must hold on to their client's attention spans for as long as they can. If Google sees that users are staying on one of Sophia's or Jorge's pages for a long time, their 'organic rankings' will increase. Now this does not mean that they should write a ten-page essay on the 'About' section of their websites. Remember, if readers have to work too hard to figure out what you stand for, you already lost them, and your Google ranking will go down with you.

A good personal brand also develops a clear vision of the work you do and the trajectory your company is taking in the market. This needs to come up in your website to boost your SEO rankings. Along with this is the reality that the entrepreneur must know that they must define their audience. They must know exactly who they are selling to, and how those people will search for goods and services on Google. Once all of this is done, then the entrepreneur is better positioned to sell goods online. So below are some online strategies to boost your performance in Google's rankings.

First, coordinate all social media and marketing campaigns across the variety of mediums that you have available. Note that they don't all need to have the same content, but the 'feel' must be identical. For example, let's suppose that Jorge likes cats and he features them in his paintings and prints of Chicago. If he took a black and white photograph of a cat walking down an alley in Chicago and wants to sell it online, he must know which buyers are more likely to click on his work. This does *not* mean that he needs to display the same photograph on Instagram, Facebook, and

Twitter. However, if his general theme of cats is prevalent throughout all of his prints and photographs, then it is in his best interest to have this theme across all social media platforms, along with his logo. Here's an example: think of the Coca-Cola logo? You likely cannot draw it out perfectly, but you would recognize it if you saw it. Jorge and Sophia have to simultaneously work on their 'theme' online to compete with other vendors. Again, this does not mean that he needs to put the same content across all social media pages, but it does mean that they must all have the same common theme.

Let's imagine that Jorge has a younger audience on Instagram than on Facebook. If he notes that this has historically been the case, then he would post more expensive prints and photos on his Facebook page and less expensive items on Instagram. He may lead them to different links on his website, rather than the generic homepage. However, Jorge's theme of vintage art prints (and possibly cats) should be themed across all of his posts and social media platforms. In these scenarios, they may be shown as logos or in the corner of his work. As the reader can tell, we are slowly drifting toward the most important part of SEO—the content of whatever you are posting.

CHAPTER 3: CONTENT

There are two broad types of marketing online: content marketing and influencer marketing. This chapter will analyze the differences between these types of marketing so that the reader may have a decent grasp of both. As previously mentioned, SEO strategies may help you optimize your webpage, but ultimately what gets you the sales is content marketing. According to the standard definition (predictably found through Google's featured snippet), **content marketing** is a type of marketing that involves the creation and sharing of online material (such as videos, blogs, and social media posts) that does not explicitly promote a brand but is intended to stimulate interest in its products or services. Unlike traditional marketing that is simply trying to sell you stuff, content marketing is trying to show the buyer valuable and relevant content. There is no shortage of people trying to sell things online, so the most efficient way (so far) to grab their attention and get them to hit the 'buy' button on their computer is through content.

Consumers know when they are being marketed to. Sometimes users search online for a specific product, such as soy candles, and expect to see vendors marketing their candles to them, as Sophia would through ads. However, there are multiple other strategies to increase product and brand awareness to drive your bottom line through content marketing. Here are some real-life examples. Rip Curl is one of the most recognized names in the surfing world, with their brand being popular in both the United States and Europe. Through a simple glance at their website, it's clear that this company is passionate about surfboards. Additionally, and related to content marketing, Rip Curl sends out an e-newsletter known as *The Search*. Interestingly enough, instead of seeking to sell surfboards to customers through this newsletter, this company is simply telling stories of big waves and lifestyle hacks that may appeal to their surfing customers. The creation of stories, legends, tips and tricks on how to ride the perfect wave, combined with edgy photographs give this newsletter an appealing look, even to non-surfing crowds. *This* is content marketing. The reader is receiving solid information about surfing lifestyles, without explicitly being marketed to. Their surfboards are featured throughout Rip Curl's newsletter, but the viewer can hardly see them. This very subtle strategy is classic content marketing.

Another example is Patagonia, an outdoors clothing company dedicated to fabricating environmentally friendly sporting clothes. Their newsletters and brochures feature a variety of stories of people engaging in environmentally friendly travel and volunteering. They even have a loosely connected Patagonia Action Works, where volunteers can get together and tackle environmental challenges in their community. Other newsletters speak about the benefits of regenerative and organic agriculture, while yet others have recipes for camping trips and rock-climbing nutrition. Now remember, that Patagonia is a *clothing* store. Their products may be related to mountain climbing and camping, but they surely do not sell nutrition guides or make much profit off of recipe books. What they are selling is the outdoor *lifestyle*. By telling stories of mountain climbers in the Rockies, guitarists camping in the woods, and how to correctly peel a mango, this clothing store is branding their lifestyle to their customers. Even their name of *Patagonia* rings of climbing mountains in Argentina. The founder of Patagonia, Yvon Chouinard, further noted that "the tradition and culture of food have always been important to us at Patagonia. What we eat does more than just fill our stomachs and nourish our bodies; good food lifts our spirits and helps us understand the world a little better." Again, they are talking about food, but Patagonia is a clothing store. So how can online producers develop content marketing strategies?

If *Curious Jorge* or *Soyphia's Candles* wish to generate a much more loyal following, they would do well to develop and content marketing strategy for their customers. The reader should remember that there are a few rules to clean and honest content marketing. First, the content must be relevant to their (very) specific audiences. For example, Jorge can market stories of local artists, reviews of paintings, with blogs and vlogs (video logs) of different types of paints and mediums he likes to use when he paints. He may also feature different aspects of Chicago or different photographic styles. Furthermore, Jorge can create blogs informing his audience of the pros and cons of different types of cameras that he is using to photograph the streets of Chicago.[17] Notice how all of these themes are related to his vocation of painting, but they are not selling his products. As Jorge knows, the content must be relevant to the products he is selling, in this case, artwork, but they are *not* his artwork. Second, Jorge must show his passion for his vocation through this type of content marketing. He must show that he cares about the painting and photography industries more than he cares about selling his product. He wants to show that his passion for artwork exceeds the profits he makes from selling his paintings online. Finally, Jorge must make a link between the content and his artwork. Initially, one may think that this runs contrary to content marketing, but it does not. In the same way, Patagonia cares about the diets of hikers, Jorge must care about the type of alleyway found in Chicago's streets and the type of chemicals used in paint. The reader will notice that though Jorge is discussing paint and Chicago cityscapes, in reality, he is marketing his artwork through discussing other topics.

So how does Jorge develop content marketing strategies for his artwork website? He must remember the lessons he learned about SEO from the first chapter. First, remember that Google takes advantage of the most popular words and phrases in their rankings to classify which websites hit the top pages of their results. This means that if Jorge is going to be getting a boost from his content marketing, he

---

[17] A clever extension of this would be to tag the camera companies, such as Olympus or Canon, to see if they can develop a rapport with Jorge and his company. This would further increase exposure to Jorge's brand and ideally create a more loyal following of customers for *Curious Jorge*.

should use the most popular and effective SEO words and phrases. As fabricated in the first chapter, let's suppose that the phrase 'vintage Chicago' is more popular than 'Chicago at night.' If this is the case, Jorge can determine which content marketing strategy he can develop through the most popular keywords and phrases. So, Jorge can create his content based off of the most popular SEO words. For example, he can create a themed e-newsletter discussing why he likes to photograph Chicago at twilight or what he looks for when he buys vintage prints of other artists. He can discuss certain themes, such as why cats appear in his artwork and use these keywords and phrases to increase his SEO strategy.

Jorge can use different types of content marketing. While we have discussed newsletters and e-newsletters, there are multiple strategies one can take to increase their content marketing. Let's take a look at what Sophia can do with her *Soyphia's Candles* small business. She can display many different types of wick trimmers (yes, these exist) on her site, despite the fact that she doesn't sell this product. She can do vlogs and blogs describing how to use these properly and describe which ones she prefers. Sophia can additionally write a blog on how different scents affect candles, complete with pictures of her candles (though not overtly obvious). In this vein, Sophia can even do a chemistry vlog on how different chemicals create different scents in waxes. She would do well to remember that Google's AI system can recognize videos, but it is still in its nascent stages. This means that any candles she puts in her vlog should *look* like a candle, and not as another shape.

Content marketing shows the specific audience that Jorge and Sophia have an absolute passion for what they do. Just as in fiction, real-life companies have observed an increase in their ROI when it comes to content marketing. Instead of displaying products, content marketing creates a lifestyle around those products. This lifestyle comes through in social media posts, blogs, vlogs, pictures, and paintings. Through content marketing, companies, such as REI, Intrepid Travel, Rolex, and John Deere, have seen explosions in ROI over the years. If the reader wants to find clever content marketing strategies, the author suggests studying these three companies, all in different industries and selling widely different products. John Deere, specifically, is known for its content marketing through its longstanding magazine, *The Furrow*. Beyond ROI, content marketing creates loyalty around a brand that cannot be found through traditional marketing means. Let's be real: Sophia needs repeat customers if she is going to stay in business, as candles are not that expensive and she needs to make a living off of selling this product.

We saved the best "pro" of content marketing for last. Content marketing shows that Jorge and Sophia are in their industry for the long term. Consumers *love* this. We all know that one magazine of *The Furrow* will not boost John Deere sales in the next quarter. However, continuous content marketing talking about the agricultural lifestyle in the Midwest or giving tips on how to harvest wheat more efficiently in Kansas truly develops loyalty to a brand. Consumers reading this journal understand that John Deere cares for the lifestyle, and furthermore, comprehend that they are not being marketed to, as their products do not show up in the magazine. By the way, *The Furrow* is the oldest type of content marketing of its kind and has been around since 1897, with John Deere consumers loyally buying their products, generation after generation. That is the power of content marketing. If you are in it for a quick buck, this is probably not for you, but if you want to show that you are in business for the long term, content marketing is a solid avenue for consideration. In case you were wondering, the latest edition of *The Furrow* talks about how to help a fellow neighbor or family member who is suffering from depression. They offer counseling advice and point the way forward for those who need psychological or therapeutic help. While the photos in the magazine illustrate country vibes and Midwest culture, there is not a tractor to be seen. However, every reader knows that John Deere is behind the curtain, and they will continue buying these products because they see that this company cares for them.

By now, the reader should be able to clearly determine what the best type of content marketing is for their specific brand, be it a blog, product website, or a social media page. However, there is a different type of marketing available online that may also increase your ROI. Remember that these marketing strategies work best when done in tandem with SEO strategies. With this realization in mind, Jorge and Sophia would be using the most popular SEO keywords in their content marketing and influencer marketing. This chapter will now look at how influencer marketing can help shape your overall SEO strategy.

Influencer Marketing

Influencer Marketing is a specific type of marketing whereby an influencer promotes a brand's products or services through various media outlets. These outlets can be online, as in social media, or through traditional advertisements. While the reader may be thinking that the influencer must be in the industry the product or service is in, this is not always the case. A classic example of influencer marketing is Tiger Woods displaying a TAG Heuer luxury watch. Generally speaking, golf and watches do not necessarily go together, but since Tiger Woods is a celebrity, TAG Heuer can increase their exposure through him. So, what do Tiger Woods and TAG Heuer have in common? Well, the watch company knows perfectly well that their product is on the expensive side, with the cheapest watches setting the buyer back around $1000. Furthermore, TAG Heuer understands that golf is a 'richer' sport, so to speak, as generally wealthier folks prefer to play golf. This means that there is overlap between their product and Tiger Woods. As we can see, even though the overlap between product and influencer is spurious, it is enough to generate an increase in TAG Heuer's ROI over time.

Let's be clear; you do not need a celebrity to influence

the marketing of your product. While celebrity endorsements are beneficial, they rarely care to be endorsed by smaller-scale companies. While Nike, Rolex, and Gatorade can afford to spend millions on celebrity endorsements, fictional Jorge and Sophia cannot. Rather, influencer marketing requires the support of an expert in a niche market. Let's suppose that Sophia would like to use influencer marketing to support her nascent soy candle business. She clearly does not have the capital to pay for Martha Stewart to display her candles. However, Sophia can team up with wick producers and explain to their customers the difference between Sophia's wicks and other varieties. She can also contact wax producers that she can use to describe what their process is to produce the best smelling soy candle waxes. Again, she can even contact soy farmers and describe the process the soybeans take from being harvested to ending up in candles. Common to all influencers is that they are seen as experts in the field they are talking about. This is in stark contrast to celebrity endorsements, who may know a lot about a specific topic, such as Tiger Woods knowing a lot about golf, but may lack knowledge about the product itself. Tiger Woods likely isn't a closet horologist (watchmaker), though he may appreciate the luxury watches TAG Heuer produce.

Let's look at how Jorge can use influencer marketing to boost his artwork in Chicago. Of course, he would benefit from a celebrity endorsement, such as the mayor of Chicago or the case from *Chicago Fire*, but he probably doesn't have these contacts readily available. However, he can use local art stores to describe how their paints blend really well in his artwork and describe how Jorge's vintage Chicago prints hang in their studios. Since Jorge likely has many cameras and lenses to capture specific angles of Chicago, he probably has a good relationship with several camera shops in his neighborhood. He may do blogs and videos sponsoring specific lenses and cameras for them. These types of reviews can be found in social media and in e-newsletters. In return, they can feature his artwork in email blasts, their social media pages, and so on. This type of symbiotically relationship helps both Jorge with his artwork, and the camera shops sell cameras and lenses.

Electing an influencer is an important decision for your website, as your product is featured by them. Professionalism and integrity are key here, and poor influencers with low levels of maturity or experience can hurt your business. Along this vein, there is a plethora of fake followers online. Perhaps one of the most frustrating parts of SEO marketing is the multitude of fake accounts pretending to be influencers. These accounts may exist in social media sites, such as Facebook or Instagram, with followers that have been bought out to increase their supposed exposure.

A clever app called InstaCheck tracks followers, blocked users, and new followers on Instagram. This can help the budding entrepreneur know if an account is a bona fide influencer or a fake account with bought Instagram profiles. If the reader is interested in securing solid influencers, some websites, such as Klear and Traackr, are useful social media intelligence sites designed to weed out fake accounts and faux influencers. However, if the reader wants a simple and easy to use formula, here it is below.

When looking for an influencer, check out all of their social media accounts and their number of followers. If an influencer has an account with tens of thousands of followers, you want to look for the average number of likes, thumbs up, or retweets they receive from their posts. An 'influencer' with fifty thousand followers and seventy 'likes' has probably bought many of those accounts, meaning that their organic traffic is much lower than what it appears to be online. The ratio is simple: find out what the average number of likes is per post and divide that number by the number of followers. Real influencers can expect from 5 to 10 percent of their fan base to like, retweet, share, or comment on a specific post depending on the type and quality of the post. Readers should be wary of accounts where less than one percent of their followers engage with their social media posts. Because building trust in influencer marketing is crucial, it is very important for entrepreneurs not to be associated with fake accounts and faux influencers. With this dire warning out of the way, let's take a look at another type of influencer marketing that is popularly used by many small and large businesses.

Another type of influencer marketing is called **customer marketing**. As the name suggests, customer marketing is a type of influencer marketing whereby the customer leaves a valid testimonial and solid review of the product in question. Think of buying a television on Amazon. Before you drop $600 (or more) on a TV, you are likely to do some research beforehand. While part of this research involves comparing and contrasting different television prices online, a solid aspect of determining which TV you want is seeing the quality differences between each product. While looking at the specs may be a way to do this, many of us go on Amazon and read the reviews left by customers associated with the products themselves. Naturally, the better the reviews are, the better the outcome for the producer. Amazon has recently done a good job in allowing reviewers to post pictures of the product as part of their reviews. Furthermore, Amazon automatically compares five-star reviews with one-star reviews to allow the consumer to compare and contrast the opinions of the buyers of a specific product. Sometimes, one-star reviews have nothing to do with the product itself, but rather the shipping or quality of customer service associated with the product.

Customer marketing goes beyond simple posts on Amazon. Jorge and Sophia can increase their brand exposure of *Curious Jorge* and *Soyphia's Candles* by creating hashtags on social media meant to increase their audience. With every candle that Sophia sells, she can add a note asking the customer to follow them on Instagram and Facebook with the hashtag #soyphiascandles. Obviously, not every customer will follow Sophia online, and many will not post, but some will. This can increase her brand exposure through independent influencer marketing by customers. Influencers, then, can be anybody who has bought the product and wants to review it online. Because they generally have no stake in the game, their opinions are treated as honest and valuable by future consumers. The beauty of customer marketing is that anybody can be a customer marketer, by leaving a review on Amazon, posting a photo with the hashtag #soyphiascandles, or doing a review of the product on YouTube. According to Forbes magazine, influencers can also gain traction on their social media accounts through reviewing your product. For example, the monetary value "of an influencer is typically calculated by the size of their social following as well as the platform they are using. On Instagram, industry experts suggest a price point of $1,000 per 100,000 followers. This price should be adjusted further depending on the reach and relevance of your influencer. On YouTube, a price point of $100 per 1,000 views is standard" (Matthew 2018).[18] This means that customer marketing can be a win-win for both the producer and consumer of the product.

Plenty of customers make a living off of reviewing different types of products online (or even playing a video game on camera). This means that Jorge and Sophia likely do not know who is an influencer when they sell them a product, meaning that customer service is always important, as a bad review from a notable influencer can really hurt their business. Naturally, not every business strategy can incorporate customer marketing as a viable means of influencer marketing. In our two examples in this book, it clearly makes much more sense for Sophia to generate exposure and a larger audience through customer marketing than Jorge. This is due to

---

[18] Quotation taken from https://www.forbes.com/sites/theyec/2018/07/30/understanding-influencer-marketing-and-why-it-is-so-effective/#488bb0d671a9.

multiple factors, and the reader will have to determine whether or not customer marketing makes sense for their business. Jorge's products are all unique, as artwork is painted *once*. Naturally, Jorge can duplicate his artwork, but as his industry is dependent on the effort he put into the paintings and pictures, the dynamic doesn't work too smoothly with customer marketing. An art patron may honestly appreciate Jorge's talent, but since every artwork is different, it makes little sense to review his work online. Sophia, on the other hand, has a relatively simple, common, and inexpensive product. These types of products lend themselves to customer marketing, especially since candles are a consumption product (they run out, and you have to buy more). In contrast to artwork, which is not consumed, Sophia is more or less guaranteed to have repeat customers if she plays her cards right and provides a solid product with good customer service. Jorge likely doesn't have too many repeat customers, meaning that his marketing strategy would be different than Sophia's.

While customer marketing is an aspect of influencer marketing, it is a much more informal (and potentially risky) approach to online marketing. Influencers, such as camera shops for Jorge, can sign a legal contract not to post negative campaigns about *Curious Jorge* on their website. However, this is not the case for consumer marketing. One bad review by a trusted consumer with thousands of Instagram and YouTube followers can absolutely destroy your business. In this sense, consumer marketing is a much more risky endeavor than traditional influencer marketing. The reader will have to decide for themselves if they wish to promote consumer marketing by the use of hashtags, customer service pitches to leave reviews on Amazon, and the like. Again, as with other types of influencer marketing, consumer marketing is subject to the same SEO rules and strategies as before. That means that it is in Sophia's best interest to pick an already popular keyword or phrase and get customers to write about it. This will drive stronger organic traffic to her website and products.

Given the information above, the reader should be able to determine what type of influencer marketing works best for their specific type of business. In order to leverage their influencer marketing strategies, entrepreneurs can focus on developing certain traits. We have already touched upon two types of traits, but they are worth revisiting. The first trait is **business-to-business (B2B)** influencer marketing. B2B is a popular type of influencer marketing whereby experts in different industries market each other's products. This allows exposure from other industries to penetrate your activities and ultimately contribute to higher sales. Conversely, **business-to-consumer (B2C)** marketing strategies are a type of influencer marketing whereby the consumer describes the product a business is selling. Many brands use this as a viable option to increase their consumer base.

If done correctly, both types of influencer marketing are beneficial to Jorge and Sophia's businesses, but studies show that referrals work differently in B2B and B2C. Marketing and advertisement companies, such as Nielson, have reported that 83% of consumers "trusted the recommendations made by their inner circle of family and friends. But more importantly, an incredible two-thirds of survey respondents (66%) stated they trusted consumer opinions posted online" (Meyer 2018).[19] Naturally, a family member giving a referral to someone holds a lot of weight—83 percent by the looks of it. But interestingly enough, two-thirds of consumers believe the reviews by a complete stranger. Jorge, Sophia, and you have to try to pick these strangers very carefully, as B2C referrals account for a high percentage of trust.

Jorge and Sophia would have to develop their own strategies contingent upon the products they sell to seek out and approach valuable influencers. Let's suppose that Jessie is an influencer when it comes to candles. She has her own YouTube channel, a Facebook account, an Instagram, and a small website where she blogs about different types of candles. Her blog online probably gets some coverage, and she can make some money off advertisements. Sophia surely has a way to get in contact with Jessie (privately ideally) through email or with a telephone number. Sophia may approach Jessie via email complimenting her on her reviews of Yankee Candle, Soy Candela, and other types of candles. She can additionally inform her that she is a soy candle vendor and would like to

---

[19] Quote taken from https://www.forbes.com/sites/forbesagencycouncil/2018/05/30/how-to-develop-and-leverage-a-successful-influencer-marketing-strategy/#615217b0258c. If you would like more information on Nielson's methodology for the survey conducted, please click on the link here: https://www.nielsen.com/us/en/insights/reports/2015/global-trust-in-advertising-2015.html

know what Jessie thinks of her products.[20] Again, this should be initially done in private as influencers do not like to be ambushed by public queries on Facebook or Instagram. In her private messages or emails to Jessie, Sophia can additionally request for her opinion of *Soyphia's Candles* first, and then, if the review is favorable, blast it online. Sophia must remember that reviews that are completely positive are not as trustworthy as those who have some slightly negative comments about them.

For example, if Jessie conducts an online review of *Soyphia's Candles* whereby she takes a video of herself describing the candle's structure, scent, and appearance wholeheartedly raving about how beautiful the candle is, viewers are likely not to trust her influence too much. However, if Jessie describes how she likes the scent of *Soyphia's Candles*, but laments that the wax runs out too quickly, or that the wick is too thick, viewers are more likely to trust her as an honest influencer. Sophia can hedge against overly favorable influencers by studying their reviews of other products. If she sees that an influencer *only* raves about certain products, then it is in Sophia's interest to not approach them as an influencer. That said, they may still buy her candles online and review them, but if Sophia can avoid these types of influencers, in the long run, she will be better off.

---

[20] As an added bonus, she can mail some candles free of charge to Jessie for her trouble. Many influencers actually want this, as they can then review the product first hand so that they can ensure that it doesn't have negative qualities that their viewers won't like. This damages not only Sophia, but also the influencer's brand and trustworthiness as well.

Here are some more tips on how to find good influencers. As always, when searching for influencers, check the ratio of 'likes' to 'followers' as many of these followers can be bought. A good influencer, just like a good entrepreneur, specializes in a certain type of product. Influencers can be film buffs, such as Ebert and Roper, whose commentary on films are both acute and noteworthy. However, if they suddenly started reviewing cars instead of movies, they would lose their credibility. Sophia does not want an influencer who reviews candles, cell phones, tractors, and jewelry. These industries have little to do with each other, and the influencer's audience is so diverse that they cannot crystalize into one coherent group. On the other hand, Sophia is probably fine if an influencer reviews candles, tea, and books. Those they may pair well together (reading a book by candlelight while sipping on tea) and may have overlapping audiences, though the influencer may not specialize in a specific industry. This is especially true if the influencer is creating an audience around a certain lifestyle of cozy fireside reading.

Sophia should also determine the type of persona she wants influencing her products. While a tough and bearded man in a flannel shirt and muddy boots with a country accent may be perfect to review John Deere tractors, that same man is likely not going to develop a solid audience reviewing *Soyphia's Candles*, talented though he may be. Personas are often hard to define, but you know it when you see it. Influencers often exaggerate their personas online to appeal to a certain audience anyway, so much of this work may be done for you, but it is good practice to be able to perfectly describe an influencer's persona before approaching them. On a general note, always avoid personas that curse, use slurs, or profanity in any way, as these influencers ultimately hurt your business. Unless you are running a raunchy comedy club or work for WrestleMania, these personas should be avoided.

Another rather unique trait that is hard to find is an influencer who uses colorful and descriptive language when describing your product. Let's imagine that there are two influencers that Sophia is looking to approach. The first influencer described another candle by saying the following: "This candle is very pretty, and I like the orange color it has. The wick is a good size, and I tested the candle – it lasts for about five hours. The smell of the candle was pumpkin spice, which is good for October and November. I also liked the casing of the candle because it is clear and it did not get burned when the candle went down." The second influencer stated something like the following: "This beautiful candle enjoys a vibrant mix of orange and yellow hues, which match perfectly with your autumn décor, reminding us of falling leaves and sweater weather. Its pumpkin spice scent makes you want to read a book by the fireplace while sipping on a pumpkin spice latte and enjoying this candle's aroma. Since this candle is made of soy, it is not only beneficial to the environment, it leaves no residue on its casing or in your home, allowing you to enjoy its scent while keeping your air clean and purified." If Sophia has to choose between these two influencers, it is in her best interest to go for the latter option, as the language they choose to describe the products far outweighs the first option.[21]

Another trait to look for in your search for influencers is the number of comments that their followers leave on their blogs, YouTube videos, and the like. This shows the entrepreneur a few things. First, it tells the entrepreneur that viewers are engaging with the influencer in a meaningful way. Are they asking the influencer more questions? Do they tend to agree with the influencer's opinions about a certain product, or are they offering a different perspective? These types of comments generate organic traffic around a product and expand the fan base of both the influencer and the seller of the product. If you are lucky, comments on a blog or video are in line with popular SEO searches. Second, when looking at comments, the small business owner should see if the influencer is responding in an efficient or professional manner. Do they seem knowledgeable about the subject both in the video and in writing? Are there consistent grammatical mistakes in their responses? Are the influencers pushing a certain product or are they guiding viewers in the right direction regarding their products? Generally, good

---

[21] Good influencers attempt to use colorful and flowery language by nature when they are describing a product. There are many tactics that influencers use to attract an audience and retain them. Just like with Jorge and Sophia, trust is paramount when it comes to influencers. Other strategies that influencers use is 'touching' the product a lot when doing a YouTube video or some other type of vlog. This is especially true with clothing and shoes, as they are attempting to show what the product is made of (less so for cars and such). For products like the pickup truck, Dodge Ram, influencers are more likely to be (or pretend to be) blue-collar men working in construction-related industries. On the other hand, an influencer describing earrings and bracelets is likely to be a woman.

influencers thank viewers for leaving comments and then provide more information rather than reiterating what was in the video or blog. Finally, look for influencers that engage with a wide audience and can pinpoint their industries very well. They may use hashtags, but may also embed different backlinks to other influencers and websites. Remember, these backlinks are extremely helpful when it comes to SEO, especially with Google constantly tinkering their algorithm to provide a better service for their users.

There are three primary and widely accepted manners in which influencers can tap into your target audience. In Sophia's case, her target audience is probably middle-class women interested in soy candles that have some expenses set out for luxuries such as these. Sophia knows perfectly well that targeting the ultra-rich likely will not work as a strategy for her business, with the same being true regarding potential customers living paycheck to paycheck and barely making ends meet. By the same token, most men cannot distinguish between soy candles and regular ones (for those men reading, soy candles don't leave black residue on the candle's glass casing).

Now that Sophia's target audience is defined, she can network with her influencer to determine the best strategy for selling her product. The primary way that influencers can boost Sophia's ROI is through social media marketing. If Jessie has her own Facebook page rating candles, she can tag Sophia asking her a poignant question about one of her products. Sophia can then wait for some commentators and likes before responding. The same can be said for blogs and

YouTube videos. These social media strategies may be a useful way of increasing brand exposure to previously unknown contacts. A caveat is in order here though: social media branding works beautifully if you have a product that is easy to ship and is the same every time you produce it. Your product or service must additionally not be locally based. For example, a wedding photographer in Toronto has little to gain from an influencer with a large presence in the United States. The same holds true for Jorge, whose product cannot be easily replicated, as all artwork is unique.

The second way an influencer can increase your brand exposure is through their own e-newsletters and physical newsletters. In our examples, Sophia can determine if Jessie has an e-newsletter by signing up for it when she goes on her website. While it is difficult to gauge how many members an influencer has in their newsletter, there are multiple ways to determine its strength as a marketing tool. Does the newsletter have hyperlinks connected to similar products? Is only one product featured per newsletter? How often are people receiving these newsletters in their email? If the answer is twice a day, most viewers are probably ignoring it, as they do not need that many soy candles! The opposite of influencer newsletters is also the case – Sophia does not need Jessie to send out newsletters on her behalf if she can quote Jessie in her own newsletters. Sophia can add links to the influencer's website, Facebook, and Instagram in order to help out the influencer while increasing the exposure of her brand.

Finally, the third way an influencer can help market a product is by sharing marketable content. This may include brief snippets of the product itself, combined with infographics and shareable blogs that boost exposure of a brand. While these may include hashtags, Sophia should make sure to check Google Analytics for the best keywords to use when tagging her content. A simple keyword, such as #soycandle may not do the trick, as it is likely that other soy candle makers are producing a similar product, and Sophia may inadvertently lead them to other producers. When creating these infographics to be shared by influencers, the budding entrepreneur can ask the audience general questions about what they like most about a product or how often they use a certain service. Feel free to get creative with your audience along this line, as they will be able to put a face behind the product. Remember, with all types of influencer marketing strategies, you want viewers to have an emotional response (ideally a good one) to your product. These emotional responses are what they will remember, and if it's good, you will have repeat and loyal buyers, which is the backbone of any small business.

The future of marketing is clearly in the Internet. Because of this, it is in the entrepreneur's best interest to engage in different types of marketing strategies. Naturally, since this book is about SEO and how Google is changing, there are multiple strategies used for generating more organic growth on an individual scale. But if you want your company to grow fast, you need to engage with others as well. This can be in the form of content marketing or influencer marketing. Depending on the industry that you are in, you may benefit from one type of marketing over another. Hopefully, the last chapter was able to shed some light on the trajectory your business marketing strategy may take in the future. Now, we will move on to a trend that was mentioned in Chapter 1 but deserves its own section—mobile marketing. As we previously noted, the fastest increases in Google searches have been coming from mobile phones rather than laptops. This next section discusses how you can optimize your marketing strategy to increase your brand exposure on mobile devices.

Google's Featured Snippet:

Google's featured snippet is the featured result that appears in a separate box above the search results for some search inquiries. This is prime real estate—the chance to be the very first thing a user sees, and likely, the answer to their question. The featured snippet is Google's best attempt to answer the question or inquiry the user searched for using the data they have from the search results they display for that search. The good news is that even if your page isn't in the top-ranking results for the query, you may still be the featured snippet which gives you a leg up on even the number 1 ranked site for that query.

An in-depth study of google search trends by SEMRUSH, indicated that over 40% of questions asked on Google included a featured snippet. This percentage will likely continue to grow in the future.

Comparison searches also garnered more than a 20% rate of results including a Featured Snippet.

Sometimes the featured snippet is a paragraph, sometimes it's a list or table. In a paragraph, you'll want to keep it succinct and direct. Typical featured Snippets are 40-60 words. If the question begs a list, you'll want to make the list longer rather than shorter. This will give the user more incentive to click on your link because google will be forced to feature only part of your list with an indication that they'll have to click on your link to see the full list.

SEMRUSH analyzed the most successful pages that earned up to 10 different results for a single page or article on their site and here's what they found:

Your domain must be secure. That is HTTPS

Your site must be mobile friendly—Snippet is most effective on mobile because people want a quick answer. If they're searching something on their desktop, they'll likely be looking for a more in-depth answer and may not focus on the snippet.

Your site should have a strong emphasis and track record of social engagement. This indicates to google that you're something of an authority or at least popular and increases the likelihood of earning a snippet.

Your site should have lots of images and visual aids or media for your content. The content should be regularly broken up by images or videos or illustrations.

Have external list citations: cite your sources of authority. This will make your answers seem more credible and established and indicate to Google that your content is reliable.

To read about SEMRUSH's study indepth, visit the article's page at https://www.semrush.com/blog/large-scale-study-how-to-rank-for-featured-snippets-in-2018/.

Generally speaking, apart from the detail-oriented features your website must/should have to earn a featured snippet, you want to focus specifically on answering the question. There's a subtlety here because you want to answer the question well enough to earn the Featured snippet, but not so well that the user doesn't need any more information and therefore doesn't click on your link to go to your site. This also means that you should choose the right kind of questions to address. These might be questions that would be answered by a list of items or answers, or questions that don't have an obvious, simple answer. These are the types of questions that will make someone click on your link because they want more information beyond the snippet.

CHAPTER 4: MOBILE MEDIA

Mobile devices are becoming more prominent in Google searches by the day. In order to keep up with this type of technological advance, the entrepreneur must ensure that their website is friendly to these devices. Just like everything on the Internet, there is a specific definition of SEO for mobile devices—**mobile optimization**. Similar to standard SEO, mobile optimization ensures that visitors to a website have an experience that is just as optimized for their mobile devices as for their desktop computers. Incredibly enough, while many sites offer stunning webpages online, their mobile optimization is completely lacking. Some websites prefer to have an app for their audiences, while others may rely on a search engine. While having your own mobile app is easy enough, the vast majority of buyers do not want yet another app that they have to download on their phones, especially if they are buying products from you once every six months or so. Because of this, it is in your best interest to ensure that your website is optimized for mobile devices.

The first thing that you should know about mobile optimization is that Google knows perfectly well that more and more users are searching for products on their cell phones. However, their traditional ranking system was focused much more on desktops and laptops.[22] Because of this, they are shifting their focus to **mobile-first indexing**. In their words, although their "search index will continue to be a single index of websites and apps, [Google's] algorithms will eventually primarily use the mobile version of a site's content to rank pages from that site, to understand structured data, and to show snippets from those pages in our results" (Google 2016).[23] Naturally, while their index will account for mobile documents, they will continue to monitor desktop and laptop use as well. Google, along with many bloggers and SEO aficionados, have some advice for optimizing your content for mobile devices. These nuggets of information are worth exploring below, as they will help you provide for the best online customer experience for your brand.

Besides their size, the first difference between desktop computers and mobile devices is page speed. Because desktop computers and laptops use Ethernet cables or Wi-Fi to connect to the Internet, the speed of their Internet connectivity is contingent upon the Wi-Fi or broadband connection available to them. This is very different for mobile devices, as they are dependent upon cell phone reception. For the entrepreneur interested in enhancing the user experience, they must account for what Google calls the **time to byte**. This term defines the time it takes for a website to download

---

[22] For the sake of this book, laptops are not considered 'mobile' though they can be moved around (technically, so can a desktop).

[23] Information taken from https://webmasters.googleblog.com/2016/11/mobile-first-indexing.html.

the first byte of data. Generally speaking, slow times correlate with poor SEO practices, while faster times mean a jump in your Google rankings. The faster your page loads in a mobile device, the more Google's algorithms detect a used page, and the higher your ranking will be. As the reader has probably guessed by now, text loads faster than photos or videos. However, having only text in your homepage for mobile devices is probably not a good idea. For this reason, one or two photos seems to be a nice compromise, with a 'brutalist' style menu of options for the user. In order to increase page speeds, simplicity is king, as Google's rankings will punish you for embedding too much information in your landing pages, as they slow down mobile devices. Additionally, if you are looking for Google to crawl your page on a mobile device, it will take Google longer to do so, therefore costing you more money than you likely budgeted for in this endeavor.

There are several applications that help you compress your files that are too big for mobile devices. Similar to those zip files from yesteryear, Gzip allows the website developer to compress files that are over a certain number of megabytes. Make sure to optimize your images so that they are not larger than they need to be. For example, if Sophia wants her landing page to have some graphics and be user-friendly, she would be better creating a simple graphic online using only a few colors and a quote about soy candles rather than embedding a photo with thousands of colors into her landing page. Pro tip: use PNGs rather than JPEGs for your photos, as they generally take up less space. PNGs are grainier for sure, but you do not need hi-definition photos on a tablet or mobile device. To continue this train of thought, other factors that slow down your download speed are pop-ups and unnecessary ads. These really mess up the user experience and slow down your pages, so it is best to limit the number of advertisements and pop-ups for mobile devices. Especially when it comes to advertising on mobile devices, there is little point in having ads above the fold, as most users are scrolling through the website rather than reading it from the top down.

The second difference between mobile devices and desktops is the design of the landing page. Whereas a website developer can get a little creative when it comes to designing a homepage for a desktop, less is more when it comes to mobile devices. There is little point to putting photographs with many colors in a landing page for mobile devices when a simple, five-color background does the trick very well. Many landing pages that are selling goods or services additionally have a tab on the left taking them to the most commonly used pages within their website. This allows them to quickly access products and services, without having to navigate throughout the entire webpage.

After all, the producer wants to sell their products — they should try to make it as easy as possible to do so on mobile platforms. As previously hinted, this minimalist style webpage building is called **brutalism**. While the term originates from architectural styles popularized in the 1950s in the United States and Europe, when it comes to website development, brutalism is a manner of website development that espouses only the simplest forms and links. This means that anything that does not need to be in the brutalist framework should not be there. For example, take a look at airline websites on your mobile device, and you will find that there are only a few links allowing the user to buy plane tickets, log in, and track flights. That's it. You don't need anything else. All websites need on mobile devices are the rich snippets of information that convey the most amount of data with the fewest words. Often, this is more art than science, but with practice, anyone can learn. This logic also holds true for blogs. Only what needs to be on the webpage should be there and in the simplest format available.

Now that we broached the subject of blogs, it is necessary to discuss the third difference between mobile devices and desktops, one that is especially important for blogs and informational websites. When a user using a desktop clicks on a particular hyperlink, they can do so with a certain degree of accuracy using a mouse. While laptops do not have a mouse, the same rules apply, as their mouse pads are generally quite accurate. However, on a mobile device, the user is forced to utilize their finger as a mouse. Because cell phones and tablets are easy to move, combined with the surprising lack of dexterity of most people, users tend to be quite clumsy when it comes to clicking on hyperlinks in their mobile devices. Because of this, website developers ought to assume that users have not only fat fingers but also poor eyesight. Hyperlinks should be far away from each other in mobile optimization. They should ideally be on the edges of the screen as well. This is done so that users are not accidentally clicking on hyperlinks when they are scrolling.

Finally, hyperlinks should not be too big (as this looks like spam) or too small (as this looks like a trick), but only slightly larger than the rest of the text. So, for example, if Sophia is using Ariel font 12 in black on her website, a hyperlink could be Ariel font 13 in blue and underlined, so the user knows that clicking on it will take them to another page.

Another characterization of mobile media is that users can travel around the world using their cellular devices. This means that if they are searching for goods or services online, then webpages should be optimized for location. This means that if you have a business that has a brick and mortar location, you should be putting your city and state in the title tags and meta descriptions of your website. Additionally, reviews are vital for local searches, meaning that B2C becomes even more important. While mega-businesses, such as Pepsi, may be physically located in one place, but sell around the world, most businesses are location specific. If this is the case for you, it is especially important to have solid references and reviews for one's business online. This may be in the form of Yelp or Google Reviews. It is also recommended to set up a review page on your website. Therefore, you "don't want to ask for reviews and then expect that your customers will be able to search for you on Google, navigate to your Google Plus Local page, and find the right link to click to leave a review. Include simple instructions for leaving a review on the page, along with a direct link to the location's Google Plus Local page"

(Gifford 2014).[24] When in doubt, assume the laziness of your customers. It is always good practice to make it easy for them to leave a review—especially if you can tell that they are happy with your customer service.

The next tip regarding location services through Google is to ensure that your brick and mortar location is found and clickable on Google Maps. There are an increasing number of users who are searching for goods and services on Google Maps, rather than through Google, as was traditionally the case. Currently, SERPs do not even need the tag 'near me' appended to the end of a search, as they know that the user is looking for a specific location. When optimizing your content for mobile searches, make sure to predict what users are looking for. For example, if Sophia has her own candle store, she can assume that users may be searching for opening times, a telephone number to call, physical address, and a list of the most popular products. She can put this information on her website, and Google is getting increasingly good at picking that information out, but there is a more direct way to display the information.

Enter Google My Business. Formerly known as Google Local, this website allows the entrepreneur to post information about their business on Google. Again, simplicity is the key here: you can claim your business, provide a business description, give an address, telephone number, other basic information, and a photograph or logo. However, you do not

---

[24] Information taken from https://moz.com/blog/everybody-needs-local-seo.

want to inundate Google with extraneous information, as this will eventually hurt your rankings. Pro tip: allow Google My Business to display your reviews on their search results, and ask customers who are happy with your service to leave a review for a discount. A big part of Google My Business is keeping your account up to date, especially regarding closing times during holidays, as one bad review on this end can hurt your ratings.

Predictably, Google has an algorithm for how it ranks local businesses. This ranking is determined by three variables, one that you can control, one that is somewhat in your control, and the last that is out of your control. The first variable is relevance. By optimizing your content online using SEO, you can increase the chances of your website being relevant to users' queries. For more information about this, check out Chapter 1. The second variable is prominence, and this variable is somewhat out of your control, though you can influence it to a degree. Prominence refers to the number and quality of positive reviews left by consumers that have bought your product or service. The higher the ratings of your business, the more prominent your business will appear in Google. Finally, the last variable is proximity. Naturally, since your business is a brick and mortar location, you cannot change this. Even those businesses that provide a service, such as plumbers or carpenters, must post a physical address for their business in Google. This is done to ensure that someone searching for 'plumbers near me' in Boston only receive results from professionals in their city, and not from Los Angeles.

There is one final benefit to localized searches on Google for the entrepreneur—there is *much* less competition locally than everywhere else on the Internet. If you are a carpenter in a suburb or small town, you likely do not have much competition around you, meaning that you can claim the top spots using SEO and localizing your content. The same holds true for thousands of professions, ranging from wedding photographers to bars and restaurants. By using Google My Business, and combining this strategy with SEO, your business will be miles ahead of its competition. This highly targeted and timely information provided to users leads to unnaturally high conversion levels, meaning that the ratio of the number of users searching for services and the number of those clicking on your website is increasingly large. Sometimes, this conversion rate can be as high as 50%, depending on the industry and users in question.

As the reader can see, some businesses benefit more from localized searches than others. A purely online business or blog has little to gain from localizing its SEO, but the small business replacing HVACs can greatly benefit from such an endeavor. You have to determine for yourself which mobile strategies work best for you and your business, as all of the ones named above do not apply to all businesses.

Conclusion

Basic SEO strategies will put your website or small business on Google's radar. By simply following some of the rudimentary rules of the industry and developing a strategy to increase your Google ranking, you will already be miles ahead of your competition. However, mastery of SEO requires a lot of attention to detail, along with keeping track of how Google is advancing in the future. This book touched upon AI strategies that Google is using to increase user experience. With this information, entrepreneurs can continue to increase their Google rankings. As discussed in Chapter 2, an alternative (or complementary) option is to engage in advertising on Google, using pay-per-click (PPC) strategies. These tactics work much quicker than organic SEO strategies but tend to be pricier, as the average entrepreneur pays $2 per click on Google. However, oscillating back and forth from SEO to PPC may be a strategy worth pursuing if you are able to pump out new products every month or so.

For companies looking to engage with a wide audience of customers and users, content marketing is probably the best long-term strategy to implement. Not only does this strategy present your customers with valuable insight and information into the lifestyle you are conveying, but it also shows them that you are invested in the long haul within the industry. Customers love this, as they know that you are passionate about the industry and are not directly marketing to them. Another strategy is influencer marketing, whereby subject matter experts talk about your product in a meaningful and professional manner. They can use their social media presence and newsletters to increase your brand exposure further and ultimately your bottom line. Contrary to popular opinion, influencer marketing goes beyond celebrity endorsements; rather this type of marketing is geared toward informing your audience about your product by using experts in that industry.

Finally, we all knew what was coming when cell phones began to have access to the Internet. In 2016, Google searches from mobile devices outstripped those from desktop computers. This means that the entrepreneur should begin taking a serious look at localizing their SEO, along with a variety of other strategies, such as simplifying their images, limiting unnecessary and distracting ads, and ensuring that hyperlinks are separated from each other.

The hope for this book is that you can first, learn a lot about how SEO works and the direction Google is taking with their algorithms (hint: artificial intelligence). Second, that the reader picks and chooses the best strategies that work for them and their business. Naturally, a business model based off blogging is going to be different from another business model selling products online. There are multiple strategies in this book that apply to all businesses seeking to increase their exposure online through SEO. Good luck in applying these concepts, and we hope that these strategies increase your online exposure and place you in that coveted real estate ranking of Google's first-page search results.

GLOSSARY

Ad Rank: one of two basic metrics to measure which advertisement gets put first in line.

Artificial Intelligence (AI): a form of machine learning designed to determine what exactly users are searching for when they type or say a keyword or phrase into their search engines.

Artificial Neuron Network (ANN): a neural system that creates artificial layers that work on different degrees of abstraction, whereby the machine would pick up different degrees of contrast and patterns in shapes, and distinguish this from white noise.

Backlink: a specific off-page SEO strategy, referring the customer to another page.

Bounce Rate: the percentage of users who visit a particular website and navigate away from the site after viewing only one page.

Brutalism: originally an architectural term popularized in the 1950s in the United States and Europe; for website development, the term refers to the espousing only the simplest forms and links.

Business-to-Business (B2B): a type of influencer marketing whereby experts in different industries market each other's products.

Business-to-Consumer (B2C): a marketing strategy that is a type of influencer marketing whereby the consumer describes the product a business is selling.

Click-Through Rate: also called click rate; the percentage of users visiting a webpage who click on a hyperlink for a particular advertisement.

Clickbait: content whose main purpose is to attract attention and encourage visitors to click on a link to a particular web page; tend to have a very high bounce rate, which, in turn, decreases Google ranking.

Cohort-based attribution: level of AI that allows the user to track returns on advertisement spending over time.

Content Marketing: a type of marketing that involves the creation and sharing of online material (such as videos, blogs, and social media posts) that does not explicitly promote a brand but is intended to stimulate interest in its products or services; shows the buyer valuable and relevant content rather than attempting to sell them products or services.

CPC Bid: the first metric used to determine an advertisement's Ad Rank; metric stands for cost-per-click bid, and measures the price advertisers pay when a user clicks on their ad.

Crawling: the process Google implements to discover new webpages.

Cross-Selling: marketing strategy whereby two complimentary products agree to sell each other's goods or services (e.g., peanut butter and jelly).

Customer Marketing: a type of influencer marketing whereby the customer leaves a valid testimonial and solid review of the product in question.

Featured snippets: select search results that are found at the top of Google's results; tend to draw much more organic traffic than Google's old model of the most commonly cited websites.

Google Analytics: a website governed by Google that tracks and reports website traffic using the Google search engine.

Google Ranking Factor (GRF): a series of variables that Google uses to 'rank' each result every time a user searches for a word or phrase.

Indexing: the process of understanding what a webpage is discussing.

Influencer Marketing: a specific type of marketing whereby an influencer promotes a brand's products or services through various media outlets; outlets may be online, as in social media, or through traditional advertisements.

Ingoing links: refer to those links that are found on other websites that direct them to one's own website.

Invisible Text: the practice of concealing information by ensuring that the text and background are the same color; considered bad practice because should a user accidentally highlight the text, they would know that the site is not trustworthy.

Keyword Stuffing: the unnecessary repetition on keywords in a website or webpage designed to trick Google into ranking that page higher.

Machine learning: also called natural language processing; AI learning from previously typed words and phrases and changing organically.

Meta Description: the phrase or sentences below the title tag; usually appears in search results under the title tag, and is oftentimes found in black under the actual website.

Mobile Optimization: an SEO strategy that ensures that visitors to a website have an experience that is just as optimized for their mobile devices as for their desktop computers.

Mobile-first indexing: Google's algorithms that will primarily use the mobile version of a site's content to rank pages from that site, to understand structured data, and to show snippets from those pages in results.

Multi-Touch Attribution: a system that tracks users' multiple clicks from one website to another, thereby tracking whether or not a social media post led to a sale.

Nofollow tag: a description telling search engines not to follow the outgoing link; Adding nofollow tags on outgoing links tells Google that the developer does not fully trust the outgoing link.

Off-Page SEO: also called off-site SEO; refers to the strategies taken outside of the website to increase the traffic (and subsequent rankings) in Google.

On-Page SEO: also called on-site SEO; the practice of optimizing each individual webpage based off of relevant traffic from search engines; refers to the content and HTML source codes that can be optimized in a page.

Outgoing links: hyperlinks meant to take the user to another webpage.

Parent Topic: a way to determine if a search can be ranked for a topic keyword.

Pay-Per-Click (PPC): also known as cost per click; a way to measure the success of advertising online whereby the advertiser pays the publisher every time a user clicks on their link.

Quality Score: a rating of the 'quality' of the keywords and PPC ads.

Ranking: also called serving; Google's attempt to discover the highest quality answers per each query or search.

Return on Investment (ROI): the amount of money generated from a specific investment minus the costs of placing an action.

Search Engine Optimization (SEO): the process by which search engines optimize webpages and websites to get traffic on their sites.

Search Engine Results Page (SERP): the landing pages for Google when a user searches for a query.

Time to byte: the time it takes for a website to download the first byte of data, with slow times correlating with poor SEO practices, while faster times mean a jump in Google rankings.

Title Tag: refers to the part of the Google search result that is shown in blue when a user has not clicked on it and turns purple after visiting the webpage.

Uniform Resource Locator (URL): the technical term for a web address, commonly beginning with 'www.'

www.ingramcontent.com/pod-product-compliance
Lightning Source LLC
Chambersburg PA
CBHW031237050326
40690CB00007B/847